I0715397

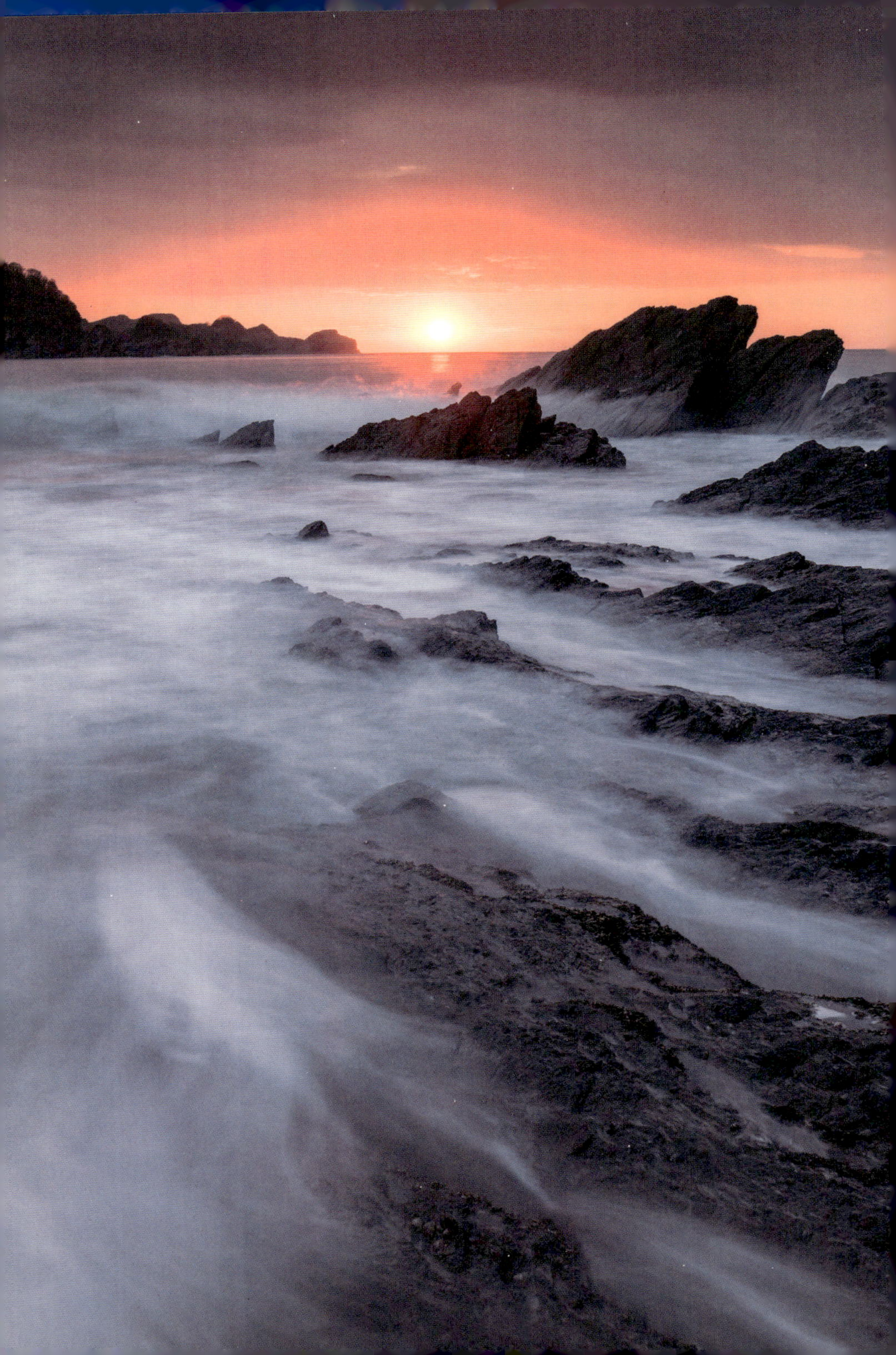

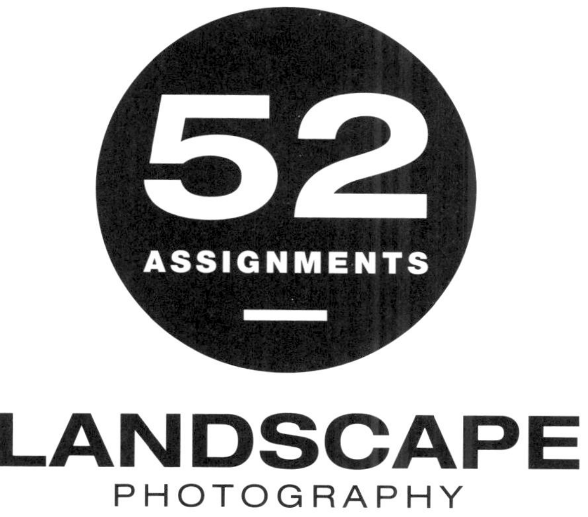

52 ASSIGNMENTS

LANDSCAPE PHOTOGRAPHY

ROSS HODDINOTT
& MARK BAUER

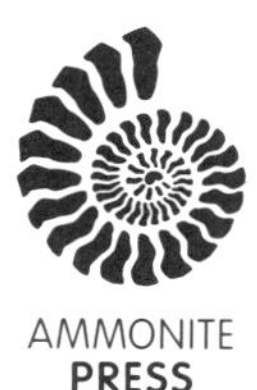

AMMONITE
PRESS

ASSIGNMENTS

Tick off your completed projects

ASSIGNMENT KEY

Each assignment has symbols showing the type of tasks involved.

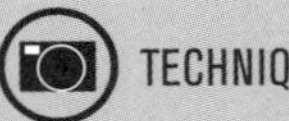

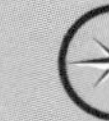

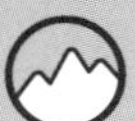

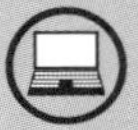

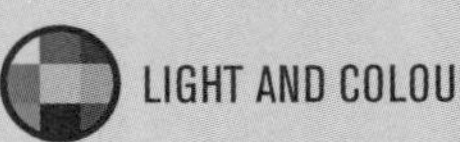

INTRODUCTION

Whether you are a newcomer to landscape photography, a hardened enthusiast, or even a seasoned professional, it is important to keep learning and to have a purpose. This is where the role and discipline of assignments comes in. It is important to step out of your comfort zone once in a while and add to your skillset, both in-camera and in post-production. Undertaking self-assignments or personal projects is key to any photographer's development and growth. The aim of these tasks is to spur creativity, assist with problem-solving, teach new techniques, and generally help you to evolve and progress in your photography. By doing so, you will become a more able, assured, and versatile photographer, capable of seeing and capturing the "standout" images we all crave.

This assignment book is intended to arm you with new ideas, and to guide and inspire you to push your landscape photography to the next level. Effectively, this is a photographic workshop in book form, aimed at injecting both solid technique and creativity into your craft.

To that end, we have set you 52 assignments, one for every week of the year. Make sure that you complete them all. Some are relatively quick and straightforward, while others are longer-term projects. But all will help broaden your horizons and keep you motivated and creative. This is absolutely essential in an age when it can sometimes feel like everything has been photographed or "done" before. Let's face it, the world is a well-photographed place, and it is becoming increasingly tricky to capture landscape images that are unique or have the ability to "wow." But remember–there is always a better shot or a fresh perspective, and it is your job to capture it…

In order to capture those special moments, you need to get outdoors, reconnect with nature, and remind yourself why you love the landscape. Dedicate time to your photography, visit new places, watch the sun rise, or stay up all night and photograph the stars! Embrace the personal challenges we've set out on these pages. Complete them at your own pace and don't feel you need to seek outside judgement. Developing technical confidence and a creative eye is the main aim, not attracting more "Likes" on social media. We hope each assignment teaches you something new, however small it might be, and that we help you on your photographic journey. Experiment, don't be scared of making mistakes, and, most important of all, have fun!

Ross Hoddinott & Mark Bauer

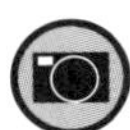

SPECIAL KIT

- Wideangle lens

- Hyperfocal distance chart
  or depth of field smartphone app

TIPS

- Set your camera up high enough when using a close foreground so that you can see over the subject.

- Consider shapes when choosing foreground subjects. Squares and rectangles tend to block the view, whereas triangles and "V" shapes pull the eye into the picture.

TO THE FORE

The essence of composition is to select elements from the scene in front of you and organize them in the image frame in a harmonious way. It is important to direct the attention of the viewer of your image into the frame and toward the main subject; or, with a landscape (which may not have a "subject" as such), to the focal point of the composition. One way to do this is by using foreground interest. The principle is simple enough: by getting in close to a foreground object with a wideangle lens, the object will loom large in the frame, with the background stretching out behind it. This enhances linear perspective and creates the impression of depth in the image.

However, there are a couple of points that you should bear in mind. For the technique to be effective, your close foreground needs to be sharp, as does your background, so controlling depth of field is vital. This is done by calculating the hyperfocal distance (see Field Notes opposite). Choosing the correct foreground subject is also critical. It can be tempting to set up in front of the nearest big boulder, but you need to select a foreground that is sympathetic to the background and helps tie the different planes together—one that invites the eye into the picture. Complementary shapes, textures, and colors will help to unify the foreground and background.

So, when working on this assignment, don't just concentrate on the technical side of things, but look for a foreground that works with the scene in front of the camera.

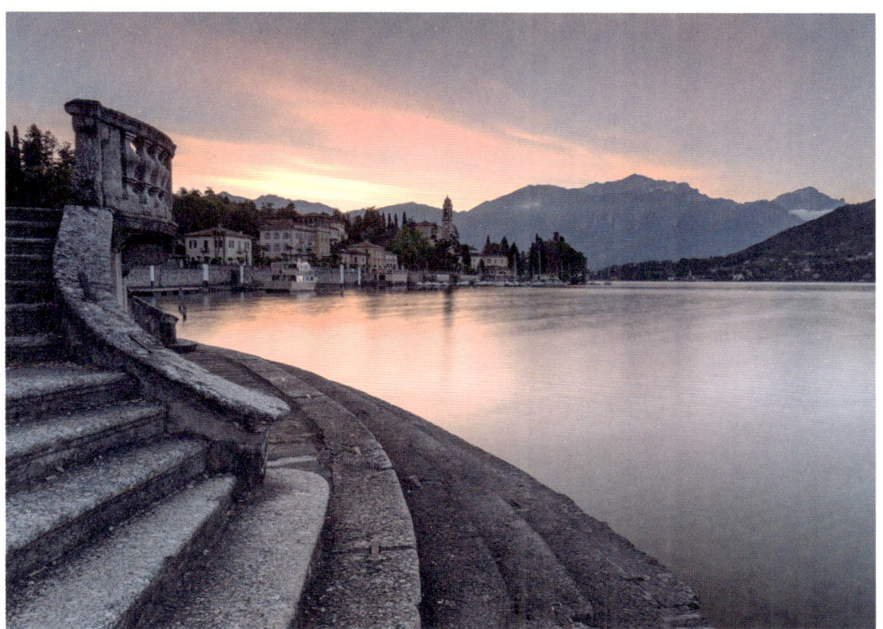

▲ *Make sure the foreground interest complements the background. Here, the steps on the shore of this Italian lake naturally lead the eye to the town in the background.*

FIELD NOTES

To maximize depth of field with close foreground interest, use a small aperture and focus at exactly the right distance. The focusing distance that gives maximum depth of field is called the hyperfocal distance, and it changes with focal length and aperture. If you focus at the hyperfocal distance, everything from half that distance to infinity will be sharp. You can find the hyperfocal distance for your camera format (for full-frame or APS-C) and focal length/aperture combination by using an app such as PhotoPills or looking online for a hyperfocal distance chart.

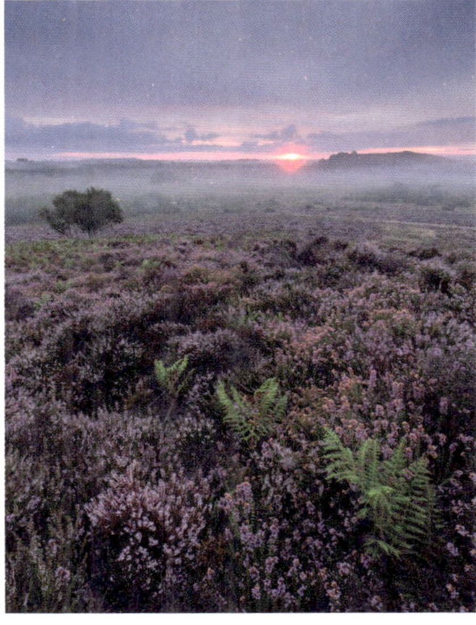

▶ *With this extremely close foreground, it was necessary to shoot at a small aperture of f/22 and set the hyperfocal distance to ensure enough front-to-back sharpness.*

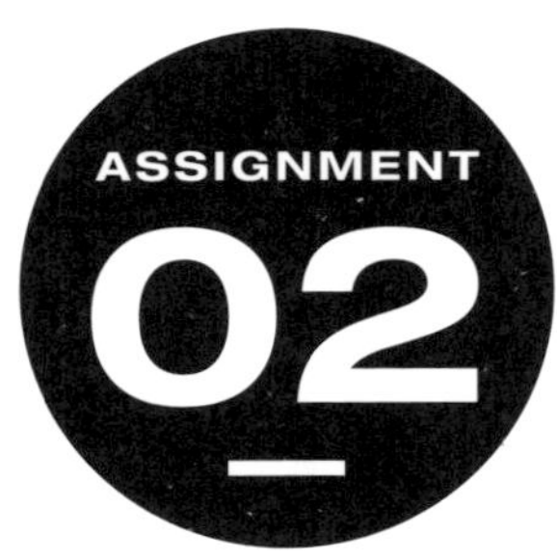

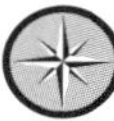

SPECIAL KIT

- Ultra-wideangle lens

TIPS

- Choose a focal length and viewpoint that emphasize lines within the landscape. Try to get close with an ultra-wideangle lens to exaggerate and stretch the size of nearby lines and distort angles.

- Placing your lead-in lines so that they enter from one of the bottom corners of the frame can prove very effective.

LEAD-IN LINES

Our eyes are designed to locate and follow lines, whether they are natural or artificial, leading us instinctively to explore the scene in an image. A lead-in line is a simple visual trick that takes advantage of this to draw and direct the viewer's gaze into the frame. For this assignment, look within different landscapes for compelling lead-in lines that you can use to add strength and depth to your composition. But be careful—if they abruptly exit the frame, they can lead the eye out of the shot instead.

The landscape is full of lines and shapes, such as meandering streams, roads, paths, walkways, jetties, slipways, crop lines, shadows, sidewalks, ropes, chains, hedges, breakwaters, and causeways. There are also many lead-in lines that are not so obvious. These can be incomplete or implied, such as a row of smooth boulders acting like stepping stones into the landscape beyond, or the backwash of a wave dragging back over pebbles on the beach. Once you start looking, you will start to identify all types of object that you can use in your composition.

Converging vertical lines are particularly photogenic, creating a "vanishing point" and a compelling sense of depth. Low viewpoints can also work well with compositional lines, but it is important to experiment with different shooting heights and angles until you achieve the visual effect you desire.

Set yourself the task of locating five different types of lead-in line within the local landscape and then use them to enhance your compositions.

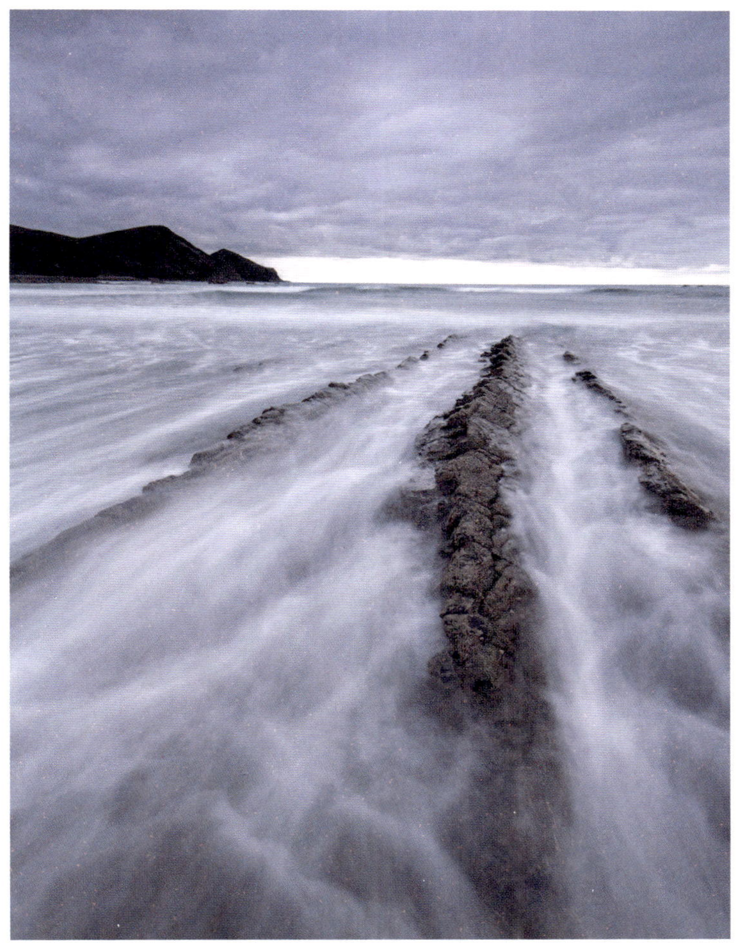

▲ *Lines are everywhere within the landscape, you just need to discover them. These rocky ledges, with the water rushing up between them, create lines that direct the eye into the scene.*

FIELD NOTES

- Lines don't have to be perfectly straight to entice the viewer's eye into shot. Look for vertical, diagonal, zigzagged, curved, or "S"-shaped lines in the landscape.

- Lead-in lines are typically at their most effective when they recede into the distance toward an actual point of interest such as a building, tree, or person, or the sun setting on the horizon.

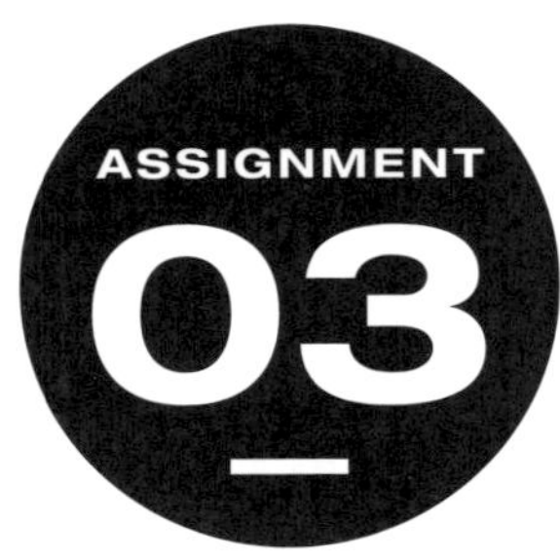

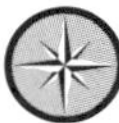

SPECIAL KIT

- Wideangle lens

TIPS

- Using a framing device often means getting close to an object in the foreground, so good depth of field is critical. Use a small aperture and set your lens to the hyperfocal distance, if necessary (see page 8).

- With architectural frames, such as archways, try to keep your camera as level as possible, so that verticals stay straight. If this isn't possible, leave lots of space around them to allow for perspective correction in post-processing.

FRAME WORK

This is another assignment that focuses very much on the basics of composition. You may have already undertaken the first two assignments, which have introduced you to some of the basic principles of composition. Another useful device in creating a harmonious image is using a "frame within a frame," where you use a natural frame, such as overhanging branches or an archway, to emphasize the focal point of your image. This technique keeps compositions tight, naturally directs attention toward the subject, and can help enhance depth in the image by separating the foreground and background.

It's not necessary to completely frame a view—framing just the top or bottom is more subtle and equally effective. When framing the bottom of a composition, look for "U" and "V" shapes, which are naturally pleasing and direct the eye gently into the scene. Subtlety is, in fact, the key to success with this technique. So, when working on this assignment, look for frames that fit naturally with the scene and blend unobtrusively with the middle distance and background.

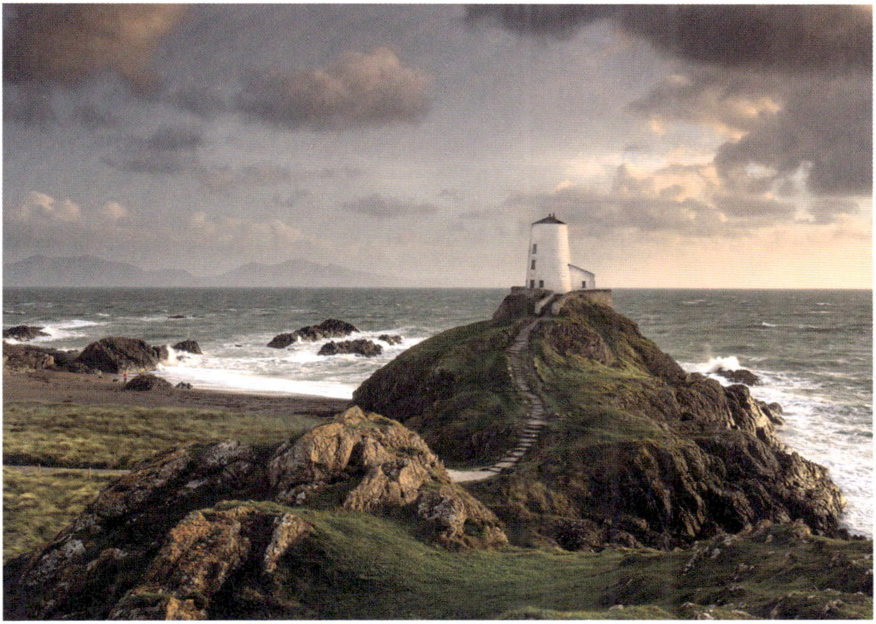

▲ *Frames can be harder to find in the case of more open, rural landscapes, but subtle use of foreground shapes can be used at the bottom of images. Waiting for the right arrangement of clouds can also help frame the main subject.*

FIELD NOTES

Once you start looking, you will see frames everywhere. In cityscapes, they tend to be obvious—arches, doorways, windows, and other architectural features. In a rural landscape, there are plenty of options for framing the bottom of an image—for instance, grasses, flowers, and gaps in rocks. For frames at the top of the image, overhanging leaves and branches can be effective, as can the right arrangement of clouds.

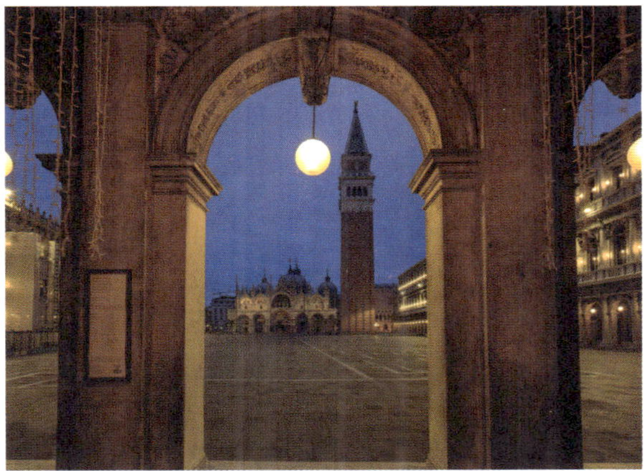

▲ *When shooting in cities, frames abound: archways, doors, windows, and other architectural features can all be put to good effect.*

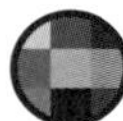

SPECIAL KIT

- Polarizing filter

TIPS

- Use a polarizing filter to enhance color saturation when shooting complementary colors.

- Colors have an emotional impact—for example, red suggests danger or excitement, whereas blue is considered calming and tranquil—so try to find compositions that work with the mood evoked by your color combinations.

COLOR COMBINATIONS

Most landscape photographers use color instinctively and, to a large extent, we are restricted in that we can't really choose colors—we have to shoot what's in front of us. However, there is some room to maneuver, in that we are able to frame compositions selectively and can seek out particular color combinations. It's therefore worth getting to grips with basic color theory before embarking on this assignment.

The color wheel opposite shows how colors work together, through the relationships between primary (pure) colors, secondary colors (two primaries combined), and tertiary colors (a primary combined with a secondary). Colors that are next to each other on the wheel are harmonious—they match well, are pleasing to the eye and appear serene. Colors on opposite sides are complementary—they contrast and have high impact, especially when they are saturated.

Warm colors (reds, yellows, and oranges) "advance," which means they appear more prominent and emphasize objects. Cool colors (blues and greens) "recede." Placing warm colors in the foreground and cool colors in the background creates an increased sense of depth in an image.

Armed with this knowledge, your assignment is to go out and shoot as many different examples of harmonious and complementary colors as you can.

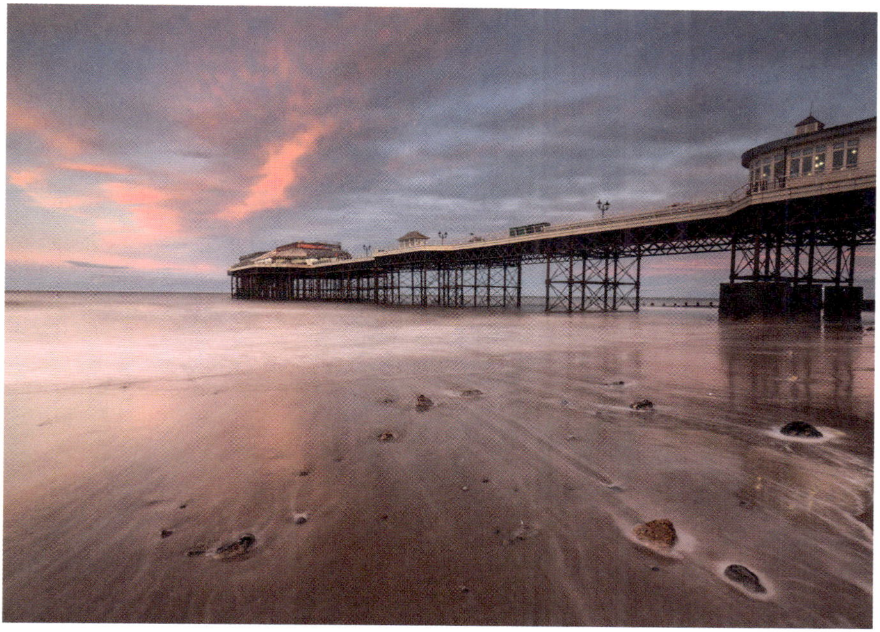

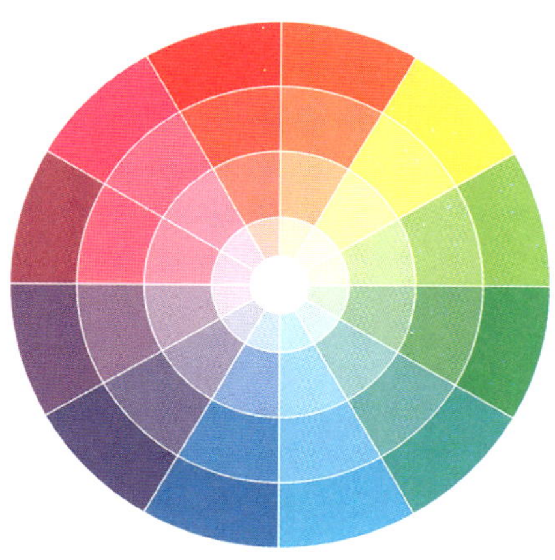

FIELD NOTES

You can control color combinations in landscape photography, just as you can control any other aspect of composition. Composition is a subtractive process, beginning with everything that is in front of you, which you then reduce using your viewpoint, lens choice, depth of field, and so on. The same is true when selecting color combinations. By choosing the right viewpoint and lens, it is often possible to juxtapose specific colors.

TIPS

- Long exposures work well with minimalist images as they smooth out the texture in water and sky.

- Experiment with different aspect ratios. Squarer ratios, such as 5:4 or 1:1, often suit minimalist compositions.

- Look for geometric lines and shapes that help with simple compositions.

- Color can distract, so look for muted tones—dull weather provides good conditions for this style.

▶ *Long exposures are not obligatory for minimalist compositions, but by smoothing the texture in water and skies, they help to reduce the image to simple shapes and lines.*

KEEP IT SIMPLE

Excluding distractions and keeping compositions as simple and straightforward as possible is always good practice in photography—it is easier to create order and a sense of structure with only the bare essentials in the frame.

The natural extension of this is Minimalism, a formal style that emerged in art and architecture in the 1960s, which pares down a composition to its essentials—usually clean, simple lines and shapes. Minimalist studies often feature just a single subject, placing emphasis on the "negative space" around it. In some examples, the negative space becomes the subject itself. This exercise aims to develop your ability to keep things as simple as possible and to hone in on the essential elements in the scene.

One approach for this assignment would be to take a single subject—for example, a tree, a barn, or a jetty—and try positioning it in different parts of the frame. Be bold with your placement: try putting the subject smack in the middle of the frame or tucked into a corner rather than on the more conventional intersection of thirds. You will probably find there is one position for the subject in which it most seems to suit the scene. Try to work out why—often it will be to do with how the subject relates to the negative space around it.

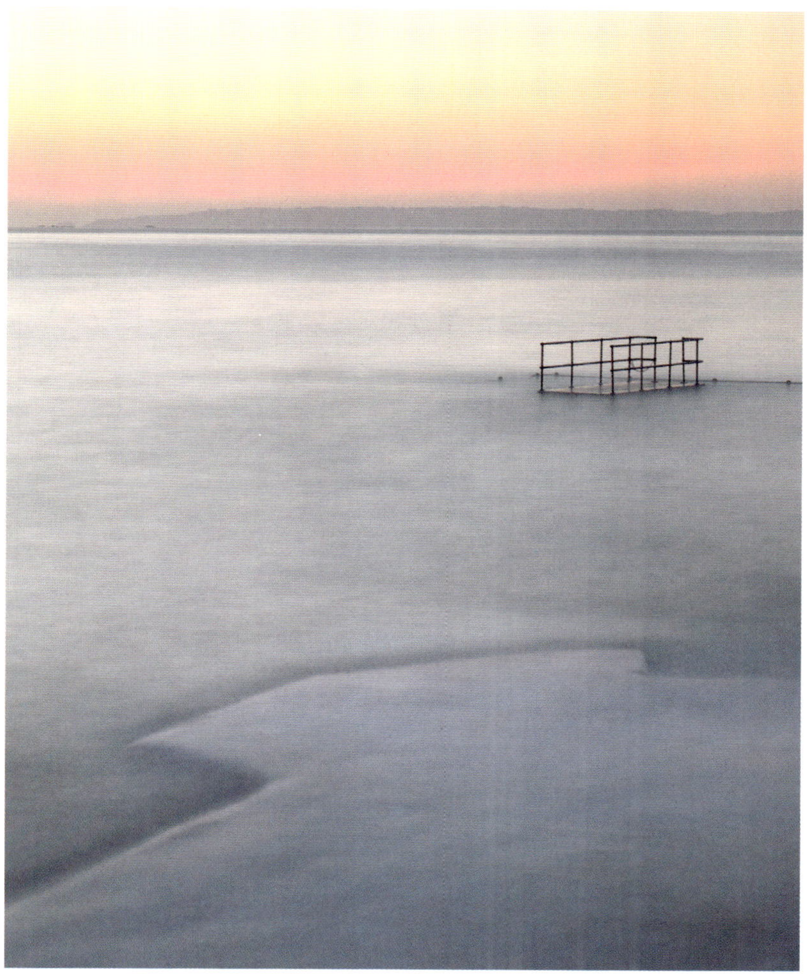

FIELD NOTES

- Use of negative space is key to successful minimalist images, often being as important as the subject itself. Make sure it forms an interesting shape around the subject and has consistent tone and texture—too much color and complex texture can introduce unwanted distractions.

- Subject choice is important. Man-made objects, such as piers or buildings, often work well, but there is also plenty of choice in the natural world. Search for objects with interesting shapes that can be isolated against a simple background.

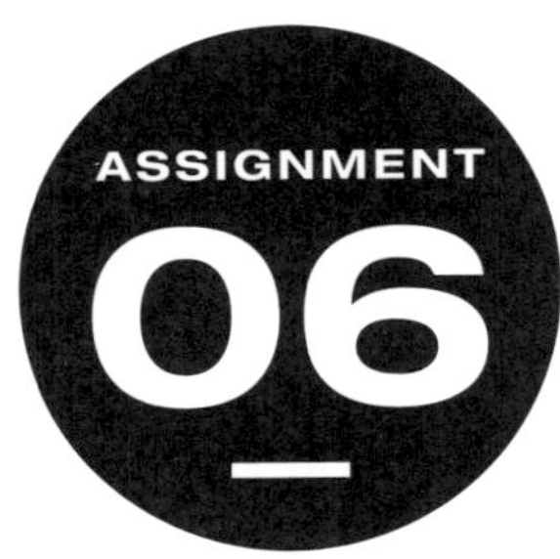

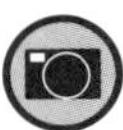

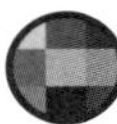
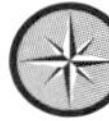

SPECIAL KIT

- Tripod

- Headlamp, flashlight

- Sun calculator and smartphone apps, such as PhotoPills

- Neutral density (ND) graduated filter

TIPS

- Light levels will be low and shutter speeds lengthy, so carry a tripod for stability.

- Use a headlamp to help you reach your viewpoint safely and set up your camera in semi-darkness.

- If your camera is struggling to focus in the low light, shine a flashlight on the point you wish to focus on to help it accurately lock on.

RISE AND SHINE

The most photogenic light typically occurs at daybreak and sunset, the so-called "golden hours." Therefore, if you want to capture quality landscapes that ooze with mood, set your alarm early. The sky can be colorful before sunrise, so for this assignment aim to arrive at your chosen viewpoint at least 30–45 minutes before sunrise. During spring and summer, this can require getting up painfully early! However, you will typically find locations are quiet—for example, sandy beaches will be free of footprints and no one will get in the way of your shots.

The light and conditions seem to alter faster at sunrise than at any other time of day, so be prepared to work quickly. Don't rush or panic, though. Good preparation will help—use a sun calculator or smartphone app to determine exactly where the sun is rising, and set up accordingly. If you wish to include the sun in your composition as it rises above the horizon, consider creating a starburst (see page 106).

If you haven't made the effort to shoot a sunrise before, you will find this a magical assignment. Watching the sun rise and golden light flood the landscape will not only allow you to capture special photos, but the experience is good for the soul, too.

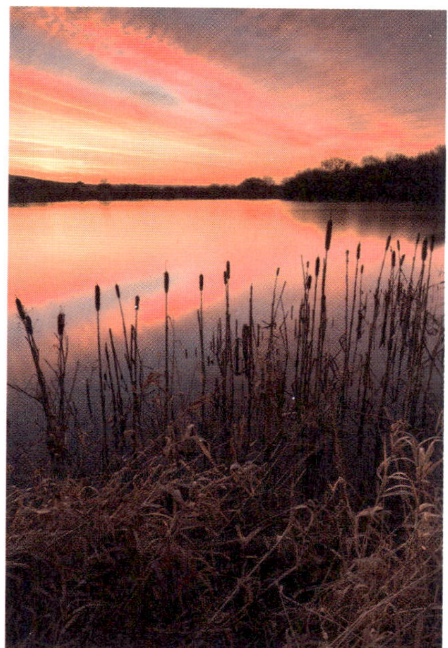

▲ *Getting up at an ungodly hour to shoot a sunrise can certainly have its rewards! It can be a magical and fulfilling experience.*

> **FIELD NOTES**
>
> - When planning your shoot, allow for traveling time and calculate how long it will take you to walk to your viewpoint and set up your camera. Give yourself extra minutes for any unforeseen hold-ups. Always aim to be on location at least 30–45 minutes before sunrise.
>
> - The weather is a key consideration: too much cloud and the sun will be obscured. However, clear, cloudless skies can prove boring. A degree of cloud helps add color, drama, and interest to your shots, so check the weather forecast.

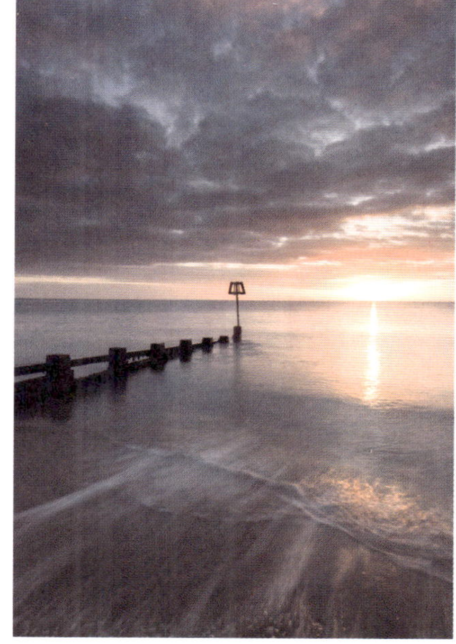

▶ *You may need to use a graduated neutral density (ND) filter at sunrise to prevent bright skies from overexposing.*

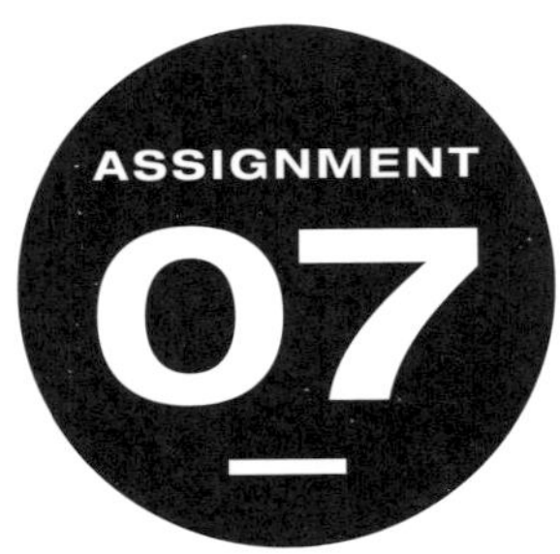

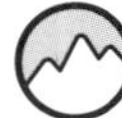
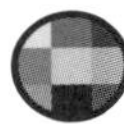
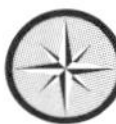

SPECIAL KIT

- Neutral density (ND) graduated filters

TIPS

- Arrive an hour or so before sunset and take your time setting up. Make sure that you are in the right position to capture a strong composition.

- As the sun reaches the horizon, the conditions may be right to create a starburst (see page 106).

- If you include the sun in your image, use a longer lens to magnify the sun in the frame. But don't look through the viewfinder directly at the sun as this can cause eye damage—use Live View instead.

- Use a graduated ND filter to avoid overexposing the bright sky—"reverse" grads are especially good for sunsets.

SHOOT A SUNSET

Who can resist a sunset? It's the day's grand finale, and with the right conditions the rich colors and dramatic lighting combine to create potentially stunning images.

Shooting a sunset might sound like a simple assignment. However, there's more to it than simply being in the right place at the right time: capturing a striking sunset successfully requires a degree of planning as well as good technique. Choosing the right location is important, and somewhere that gets the light from the setting sun is the obvious starting point, although it's not always necessary to shoot straight toward the sun at sunset—low side-lighting can be just as dramatic.

▶ *As the sun reaches the horizon, especially if it dips below a hard edge, such as a hilltop or rock, stopping the lens down (in this case to f/22) will often produce a starburst.*

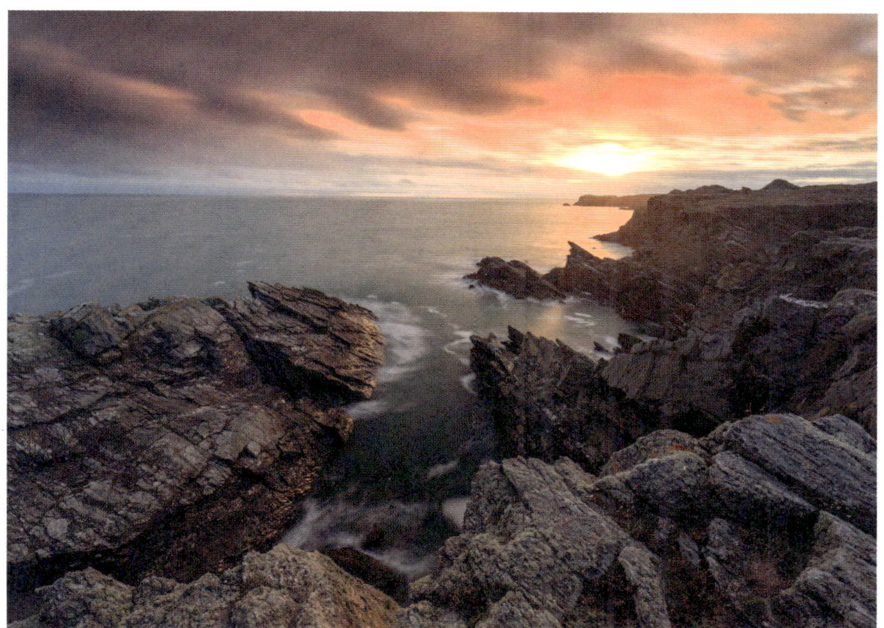

▲ *Skies can be extremely bright relative to the foreground, so graduated ND filters are often necessary to prevent the sky from overexposing. Here, with the brightest part of the scene on the horizon, a "reverse" graduated filter (one which is darkest on the horizon line and fades toward the top) was used.*

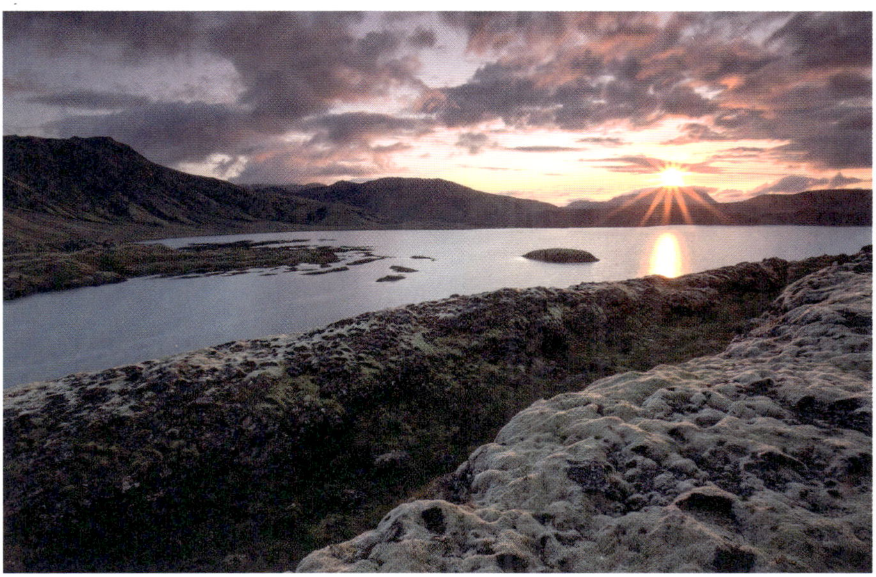

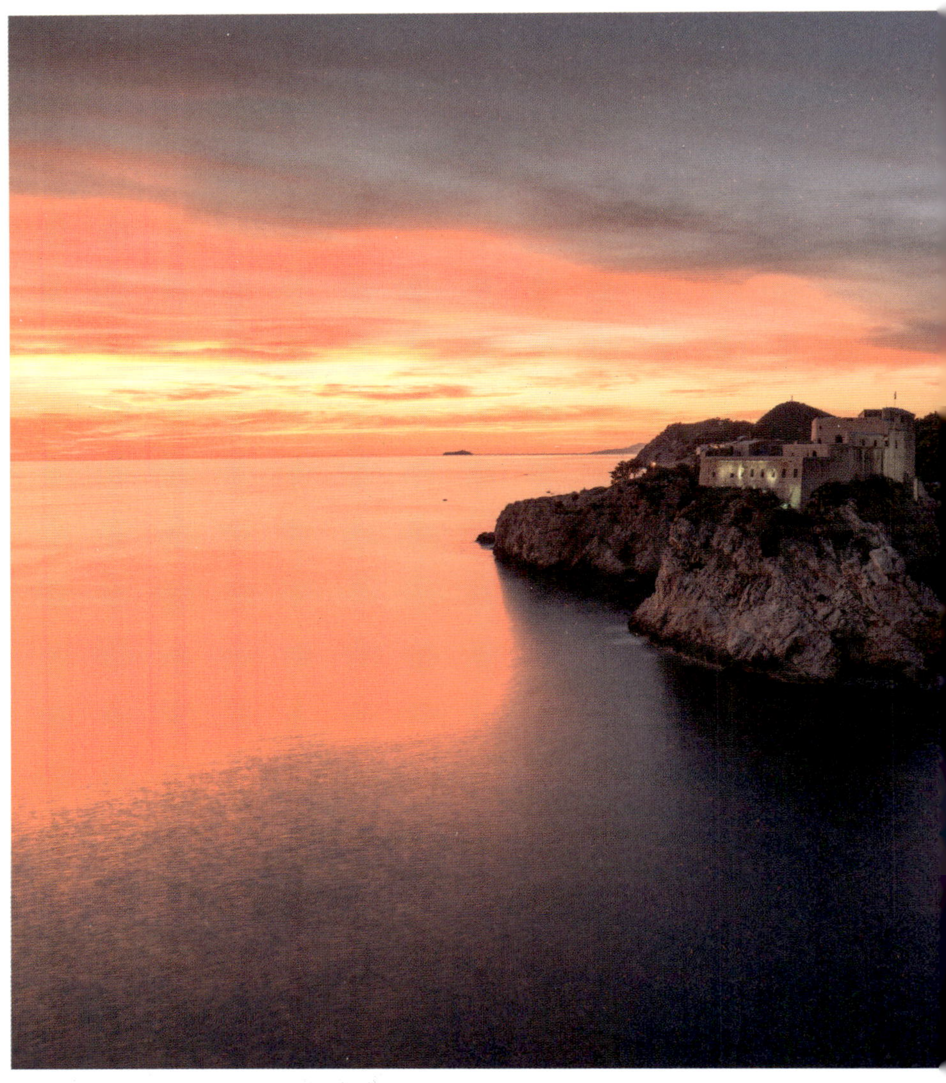

Use online resources to check the position of the sun at sunset. Depending on your geographical position, there can be a lot of variation throughout the year, meaning that even some west-facing locations won't get a good sunset all year round. Choose locations that have strong foreground interest—if there are interesting shapes in the scene, these can be used as silhouettes.

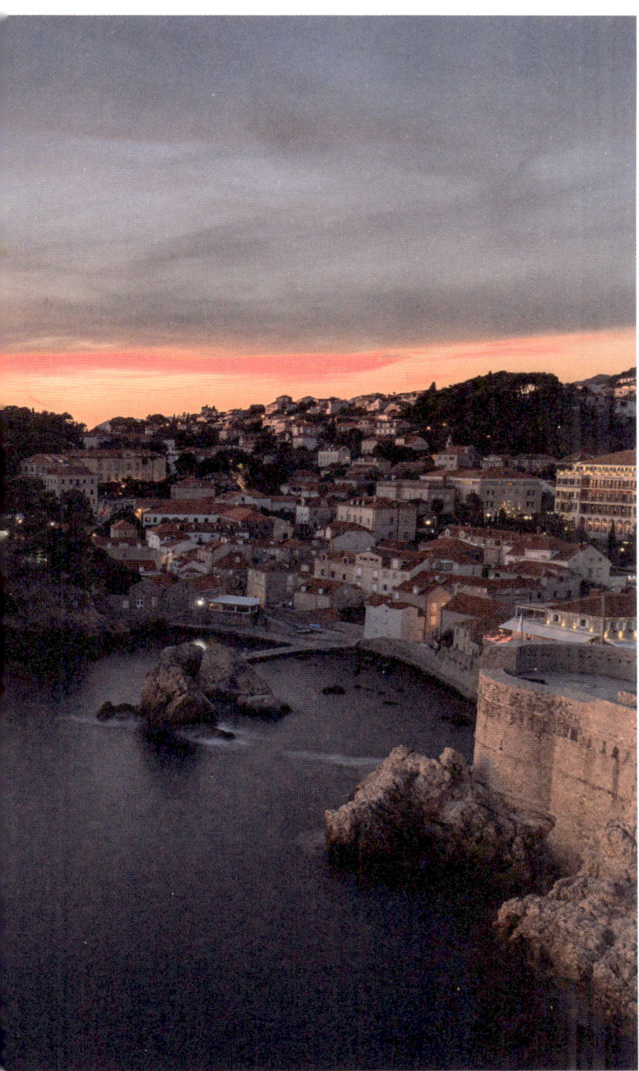

◀ *It's not necessary to shoot straight into the setting sun. Here, the sun was out of the frame, to the left, but color had radiated across the sky and the low, warm side-lighting revealed texture in the cliffs and buildings.*

Don't pack up immediately the sun dips below the horizon. The best conditions for this assignment often occur just after sunset and sometimes as late as 20–30 minutes afterward, when a warm "afterglow" can radiate across the sky.

TIPS

- If your subject is moving, make sure you use a fast enough shutter speed to prevent motion blur. This may mean raising the ISO.

- When waiting for someone to walk into frame, keep both eyes open so you can anticipate the moment and be ready.

- Consider shooting handheld (see page 52) for greater flexibility and the ability to react quickly to what may happen in front of the camera.

▶ *Without the fisherman silhouetted against the sky, this landscape would be empty and uninspiring. The figure adds not just a focal point to the shot, but also some atmosphere.*

PEOPLE POWER

More often than not, landscape photographs are devoid of people, presenting an image of the outdoors as an untouched wilderness. While such landscapes exist, the majority of the locations we visit are actually quite busy. So, we often wait for long periods for people to leave the view, or, alternatively, we clone them out of the shot in post-processing.

However, there are actually some good reasons to include people in landscape photographs. They can provide a sense of scale—the true size of mountains or trees can be very difficult to judge when seen in isolation. People can also balance a composition by providing a focal point in an image, or, if they are facing the right way, can direct attention to the focal point. Finally, people can bring a landscape to life and help to tell a story—a lone hiker walking up a track, for example, can suggest mystery and adventure.

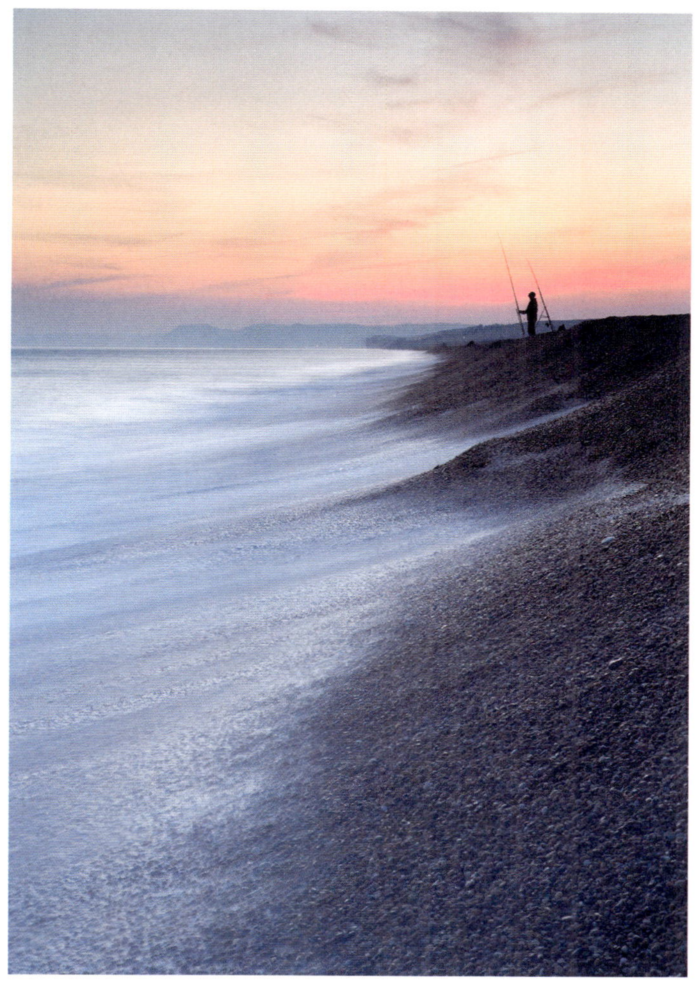

FIELD NOTES

Timing is important when including people in your landscapes—you want them in the right part of the frame, looking the right way, and perhaps even at a specific object. They may be moving, especially if they are running or cycling, and the ideal moment might only last for a fraction of a second. So, try to predict where they are going, and know where in the frame you'd ideally like them and when they are likely to arrive there. Have your composition framed—with focus, filtration, and exposure set—and be ready to fire the shutter.

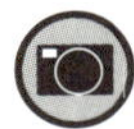
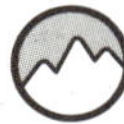

SPECIAL KIT

- Tripod
- Remote shutter release
- Neutral density (ND) filters
- Smartphone app, such as PhotoPills

TIPS

- Avoid Auto ISO when using ND filters or shooting in low light.
- A sturdy tripod is essential and triggering the shutter remotely will eliminate the risk of any camera shake; use a remote shutter release or set your camera's self-timer.
- Focus and frame your shot before attaching your ND filters.

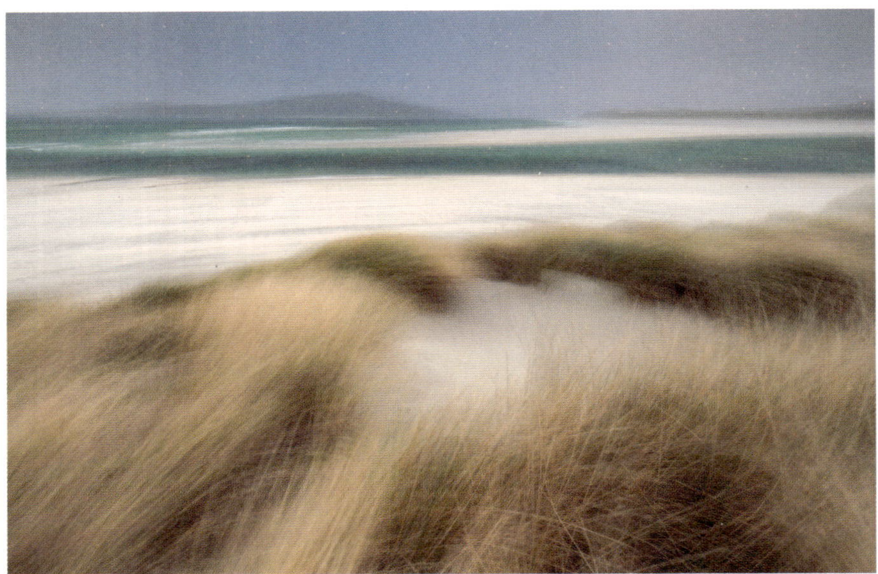

GO SLOW

Cameras today can offer shutter speeds of up to 1/8000 sec. However, going slow—using an exposure of one second or more—can offer more creative options. Subjects such as moving water or clouds will blur during a long exposure, producing images that convey motion with added visual interest.

There are two ways to generate a creatively long exposure. You can shoot in low light—at dawn (see page 18) or dusk (see page 20)—when the exposure is naturally long, or you can use a neutral density (ND) filter to lengthen the exposure. These filters absorb light in various strengths, up to 15 stops, allowing you to create long exposures even in good daylight. Your camera's through-the-lens (TTL) metering will normally compensate for the filter's density, adjusting the exposure time automatically.

For this assignment, try shooting different things—such as people or vehicles—and experiment with different shutter speeds, using ND filters of varying strengths. Also try different ISO speeds to control the amount of movement recorded. What effects do you like best? Settle on your favorite subject and approach, and use them to create a portfolio of "Go Slow" photographs.

◀ *A 1 sec. exposure, combined with a small amount of intentional camera movement (see page 114), can create dreamy-looking results.*

FIELD NOTES

- Many cameras have long exposure noise reduction, which is usually activated when exposure length exceeds 8 sec. This works by making a dark frame of the same duration as your exposure. Be aware that you will be unable to take photos while this is happening. The function can be switched off via the camera's Set-up menu.

- The longest automatic exposure for most cameras is 30 sec. For exposures longer than this, you will need to select Bulb mode, which allows you to lock open the shutter for longer exposures.

- To help you calculate longer exposures using dense ND filters, use a smartphone app such as PhotoPills.

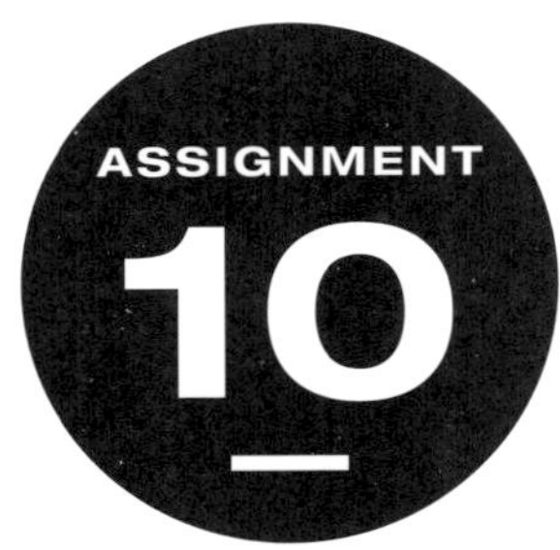

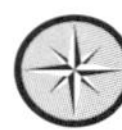

SPECIAL KIT

- Polarizing and neutral density (ND) filters

TIPS

- Try placing the horizon centrally—it can create symmetry as well as a better sense of calm.

- Attach a polarizing filter to strengthen the look of reflections in still water.

- Try using a neutral density (ND) filter to prolong exposure length and reduce, or smooth out, any ripples on the water.

REFLECTIONS

Most landscape photographers are instinctively drawn to water, with the sea, rivers, waterfalls, and lakes offering many opportunities for great images. Water can help imply motion, reflect light and color, and create mirror-like reflections. A reflective surface can dramatically enhance a landscape image, particularly at sunrise or sunset, when the color in the sky is mirrored in your foreground. Large bodies of water are best for this, but they are also more prone to ripples caused by the wind. Although gentle ripples can prove photogenic, to capture a true mirror image of the landscape you require total calm. For this assignment, you need to capture dramatic reflections in a large body of water using the techniques described overleaf.

FIELD NOTES

- Calm, still days—with a wind speed below 5mph (8kph)—are best for photographing reflections, so check the weather forecast.

- Reflections are typically darker than the main subject, so consider using a graduated ND filter to keep the light and exposure balanced.

▶ *A longer focal length has been used here to isolate areas of interest reflected in the landscape.*

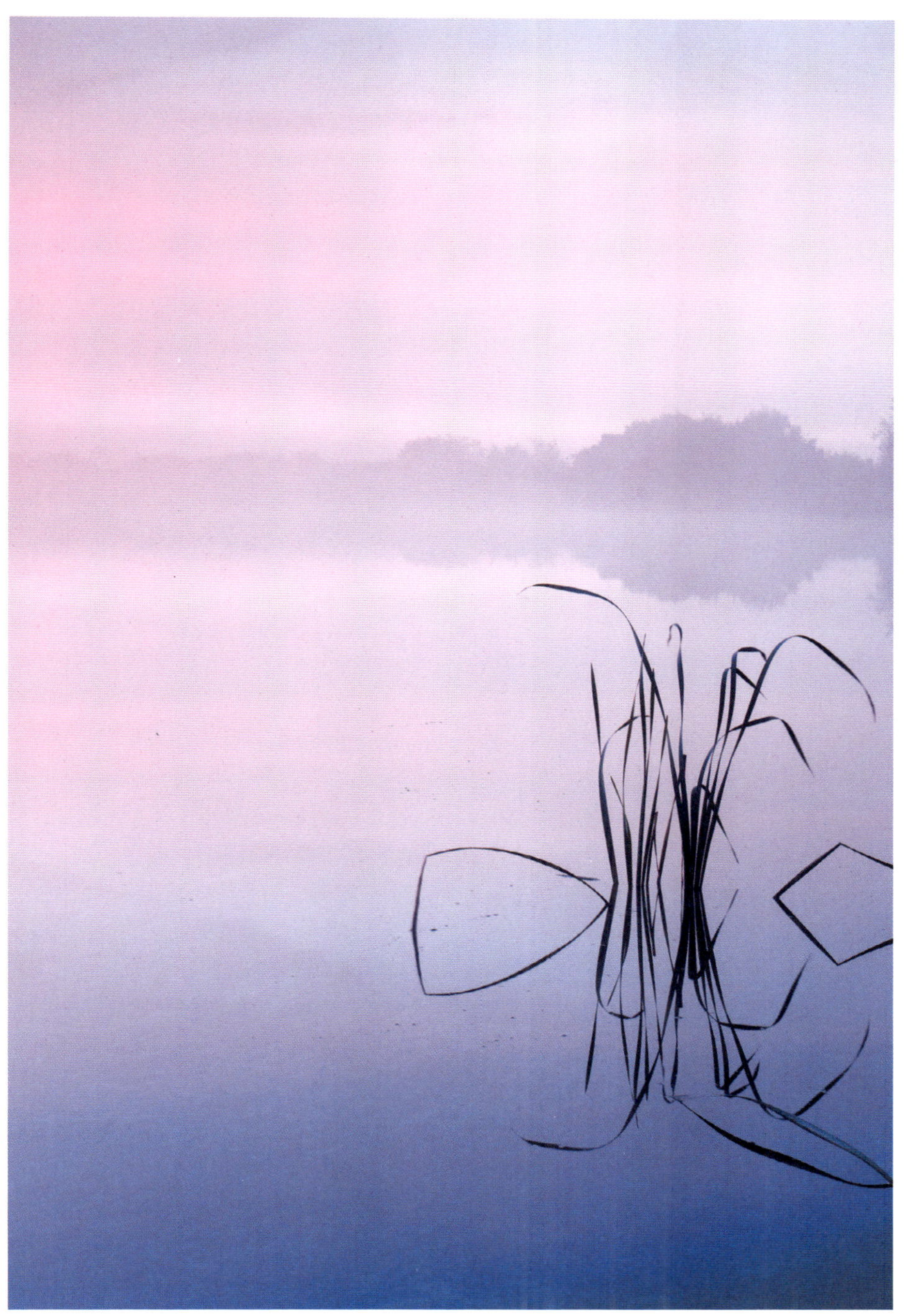

THE PROCESS

1 The first choice you need to make is the lens focal length. If you are photographing a big, mountain landscape, you will need a wideangle lens to capture both the mountain and its reflection. However, a medium telephoto is better suited to isolating a smaller area in the landscape, such as a lone tree or building, along with its reflection.

2 A low viewpoint will often accentuate reflections, so crouch or kneel down, or use a tripod at a low height. It is normally best to set up close to the water's edge.

3 Attach a polarizing filter. By rotating the filter, you can regulate reflections, and intensify them by reducing surface glare.

4 Photographers are often taught to apply the Rule of Thirds and avoid centralizing the horizon, as this can produce static-looking compositions. However, when you shoot reflections, it is often worthwhile disregarding this advice. By placing the horizon centrally, you can create a better feeling of symmetry and enhance the impact of the composition.

5 A mirror-like reflection is often all the foreground you need, but don't disregard other elements if they enhance the composition. For instance, reeds, driftwood, a jetty, rowing boats, or a few boulders in the water might help to add scale and interest. If you do decide to do this, be careful that these elements don't abruptly interrupt or overlap your reflected landscape.

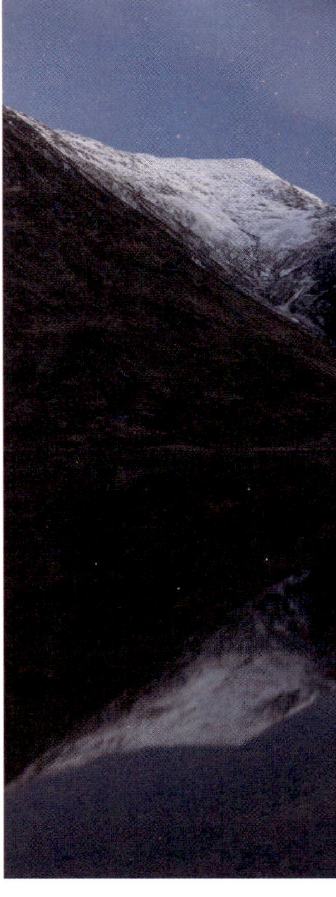

▲ *Dawn and dusk are often the best times to shoot reflections—it is generally calmer, and colors can be more intense.*

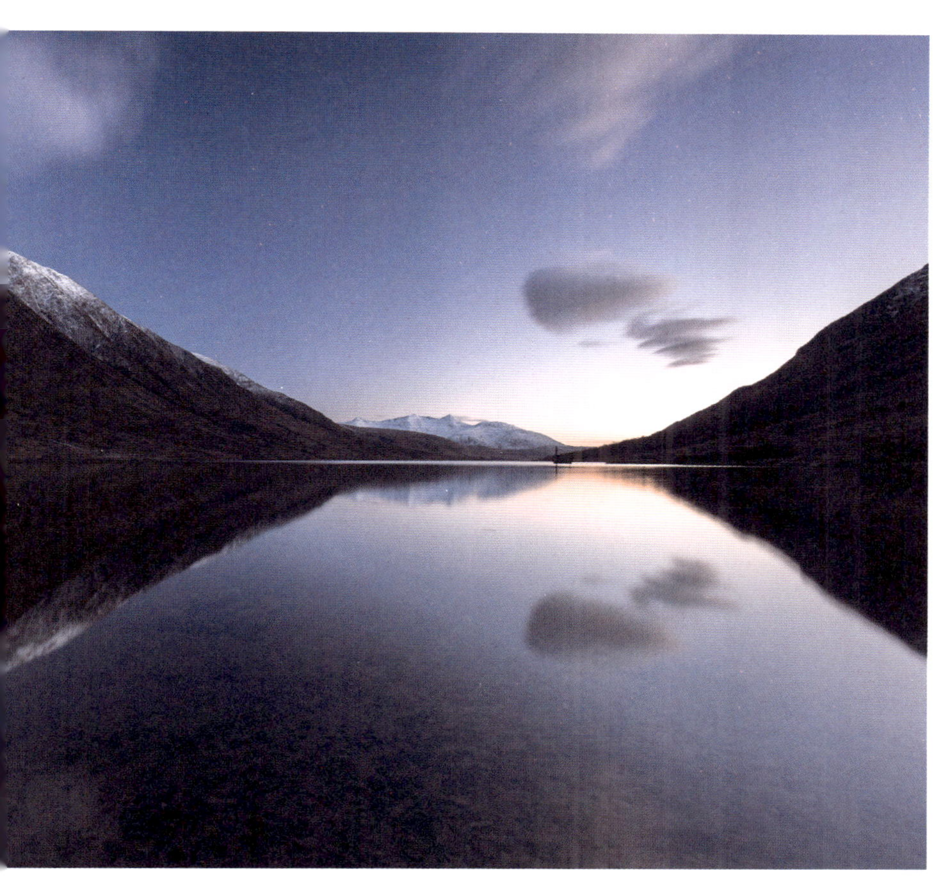

▶ A low viewpoint
helped capture the
reflection here.

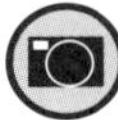

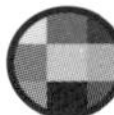

SPECIAL KIT

- Smartphone app, such as PhotoPills

TIPS

- Auto White Balance will sometimes interpret the natural blue hues of twilight as a color cast and try to "correct" it, so use your camera's Daylight preset to prevent this (see page 54).

- Although it is called the "blue hour" it usually only lasts for around 30–40 minutes (depending on the time of year and location), and the peak can last just a few minutes.

- Timing is crucial with cityscapes, as the best shots are in the short window when the ambient and artificial light are perfectly balanced.

- Start shooting just before the blue hour and continue past the peak to ensure you capture the perfect light.

- In low light, extremely long exposures may be necessary.

KIND OF BLUE

This assignment is all about capturing the "blue hour"—the period of twilight in the morning and evening when the ambient light takes on a natural blue hue. The cool tones at this time lend an atmosphere of mystery and romance to the scene. It's probably fair to say that cityscapes look their most attractive at this time. To catch the morning blue hour, you will need to be on location and set up about an hour before sunrise. For the evening blue hour, you will need to stay for 30 to 60 minutes after sunset; the extra effort is really worth it. We suggest you start with an evening blue-hour shoot as this is much easier—you can set up, spend time getting your composition fine tuned, and focus accurately while it is still light. By contrast, the morning blue hour is much more challenging, as you need to set up while it's more or less pitch black. To ensure success, you'll need to scout the location during daylight hours and decide on your composition then.

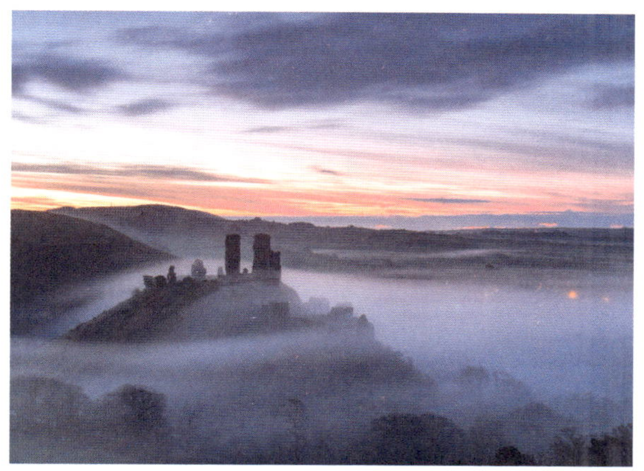

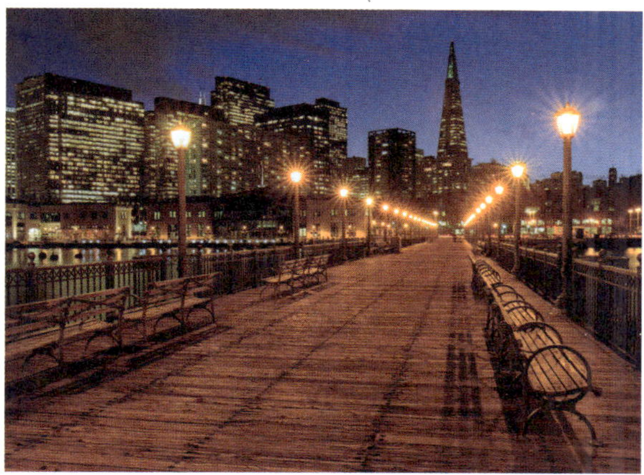
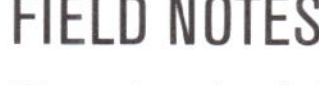

FIELD NOTES

Choosing the right subject is the key to successful blue-hour shoots. Cityscapes are a popular choice, as warm, artificial lighting contrasts dramatically with the deep blue of the sky. Prominent floodlit buildings or monuments can be placed in the frame to act as a focal point for the composition.

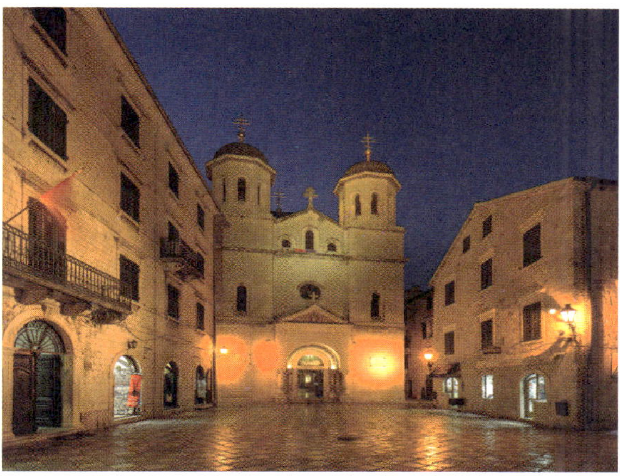

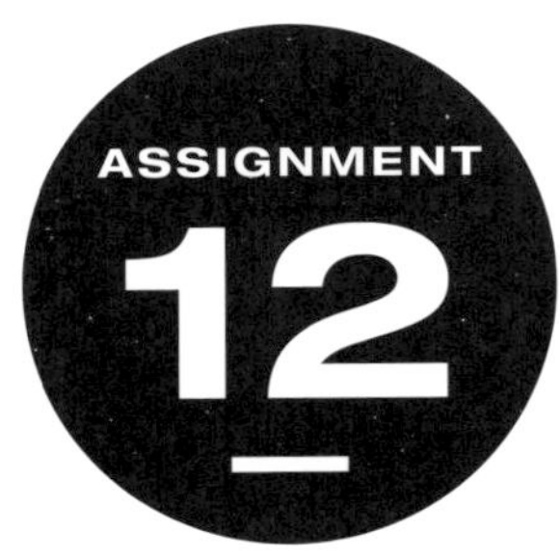

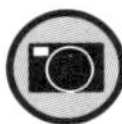

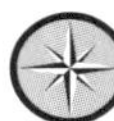

SPECIAL KIT

- Tripod

- Beanbag

TIPS

- Not all tripods allow ground-level shooting— if yours doesn't, bring a small beanbag with you to give your camera stability.

- Use your tripod's center column to raise the camera above head height. Operating your camera like this can be tricky—a small step ladder can help.

- Shooting low means that foregrounds will be very close, so controlling depth of field is essential. Use a small aperture and the hyperfocal distance (see page 8) to keep everything sharp. If this still doesn't create enough depth of field, try focus-stacking (see Pro Tip opposite).

CHANGE THE VIEW

Most photographs are shot from head height, so one very effective way to catch the viewer's attention is to break with convention and shoot from a different viewpoint— creating a "worm's eye" view of the world, for instance.

The secret to success with unconventional viewpoints is to identify the situations in which they are likely to work well. Choosing a low viewpoint can add drama by placing emphasis on the foreground and exaggerating linear perspective, but this can reduce the separation between key elements in the frame, merging foreground and background together, and reducing depth in the image. Raising the camera to shoot from a high viewpoint reveals the planes in a composition and opens up the middle distance, which can enhance a feeling of depth in an image, but if the middle distance is empty it can result in lack of structure in the composition. If you own a drone, you can elevate this part of the assignment to its highest extremes!

The task here is simple: shoot one scene that is enhanced by a low viewpoint and another that benefits from an elevated viewpoint.

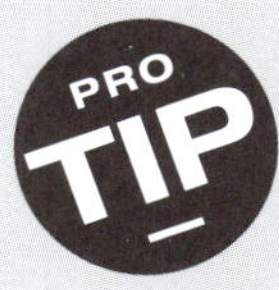

FOCUS-STACKING

This is an image-blending technique that allows you to create depth of field stretching from the immediate foreground to infinity. Shoot a series of images, focused at different points from foreground to background, with the depth of field overlapping. Open the images in Photoshop and create a stack: File > Scripts > Load Files into Stack. Select all the layers and align them: Edit > Auto-Align Layers. To blend the sharply focused parts of each layer into a single shot, click Edit > Auto-Blend Layers. Make sure the Stack Images box is checked.

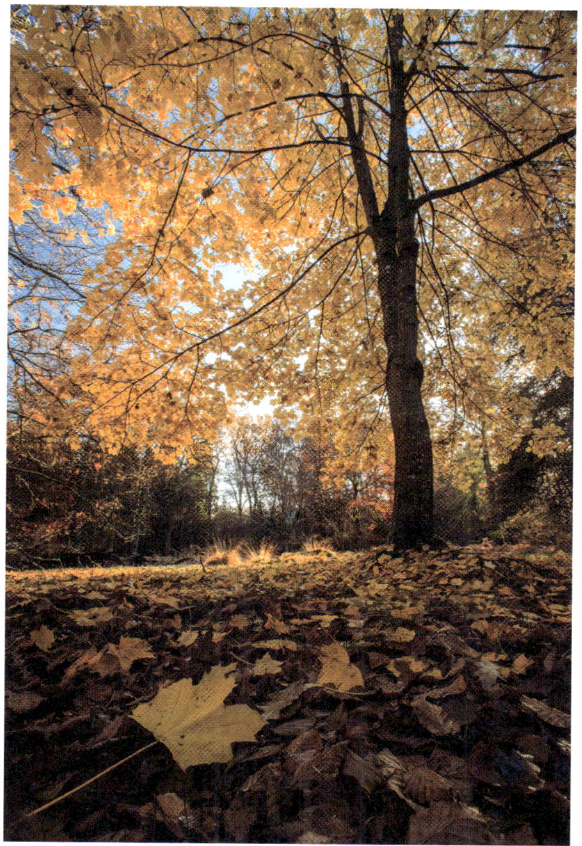

▲ *Setting up on the ground created a dramatic perspective for this fall woodland shot, with the emphasis being placed on the leaves on the forest floor and the prominent golden leaf leading into the image. Because of the low viewpoint, the backlit tree looms large in the background. An aperture of f/22 and careful focusing ensured enough depth of field.*

FIELD NOTES

It can be difficult to operate a camera that is set up either above your head or very low to the ground. Fortunately, most modern cameras have rear LCD screens that feature Live View, which means you can frame your shot and check shooting settings more easily. Even better, the majority of cameras now have tilting LCDs, which make experimenting with unconventional viewpoints even easier.

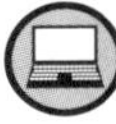

SPECIAL KIT

- Post-processing software, such as Adobe Photoshop or Lightroom

TIPS

- Avoid cropping photographs excessively. Do not discard lots of pixels and reduce image quality needlessly.

- Editing software allows you to quickly select from a choice of popular aspect ratios, or you can select "Unconstrained" to create a custom crop.

- One disadvantage of creating a custom crop is that unconventional dimensions can complicate mounting and framing your image.

CREAM OF THE CROP

The landscape is a diverse and varied place. It can be flat, hilly, mountainous, empty, or busy. Therefore, it is unrealistic to think your camera's native aspect ratio will suit every scene you shoot. Aspect ratio is the term used to describe the dimensions of an image by comparing its width and height. Most cameras have a standard aspect ratio of either 3:2 or 4:3. Some cameras allow you to alter the aspect ratio before or after taking the photograph, but many do not. Instead, you will need to crop your images during post-processing.

This assignment is intended to teach the importance of framing and choosing the aspect ratio best suited to any given scene. Cropping is not cheating, it is an important part of the compositional process: it can alter and enhance the balance and harmony of a photograph, help place greater emphasis on the main subject, or remove distractions.

Cropping is just about the most basic adjustment you can make to a photograph, but it is an important step that can make or break your composition.

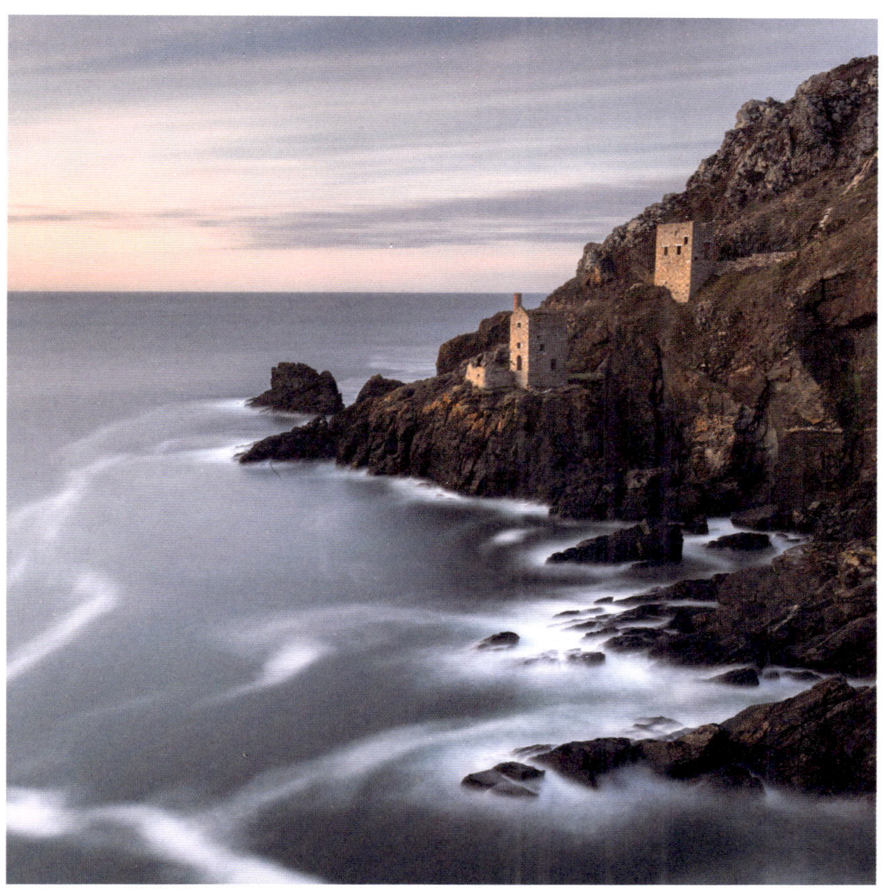

▲ *To learn which crop works best, experiment with the most popular aspect ratios. A square 1:1 format can be very bold and suit a minimalist composition (see page 16), while a panoramic 3:1 or 2:1 format enhances wide, sweeping vistas.*

FIELD NOTES

Cropping shouldn't be an afterthought to compensate for lazy composition. Instead, consider which aspect ratio will suit your shot best prior to pressing the shutter-release button. This will help you to optimize your composition to suit your intended crop.

THE PROCESS

The easiest and most precise way to crop your landscapes is during post-processing. Although Photoshop is used in this example, all editing programs have a Crop Tool.

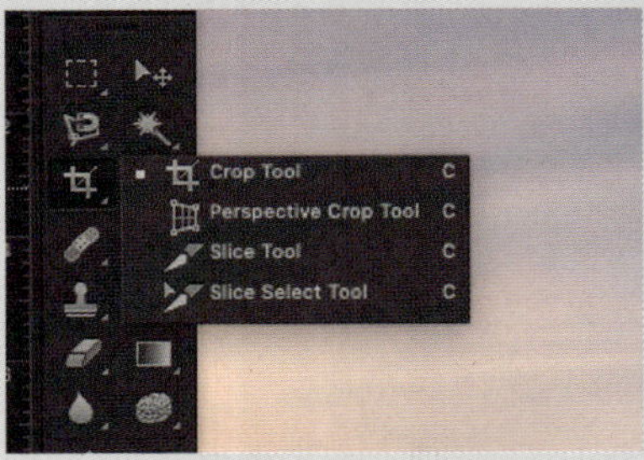

1 Open your image and click on the Crop Tool icon (the Adobe keyboard shortcut is C).

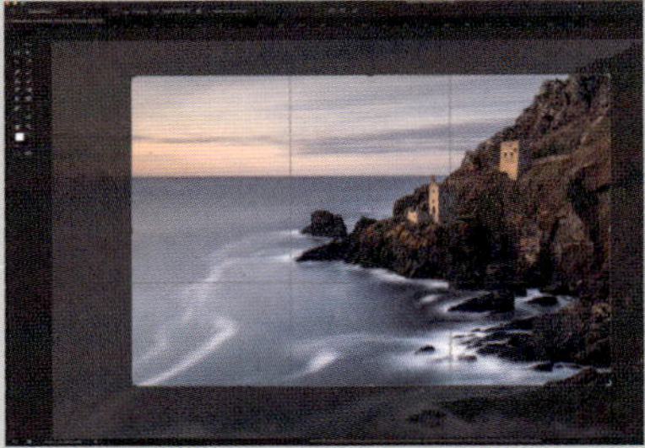

2 Crop handles will appear in each corner. Click and drag these to resize and reshape the crop box. Everything outside the box will be cropped away on completion.

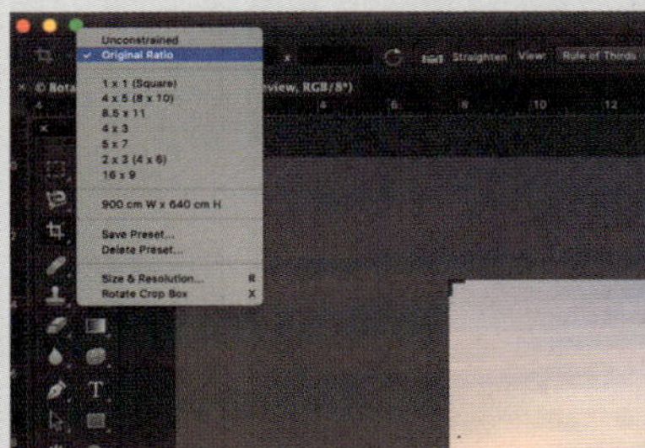

3 By default, you can adjust the handles "Unconstrained." Change this by clicking on the drop-down box in the Options bar. You can select Original Ratio or choose from a choice of popular dimensions.

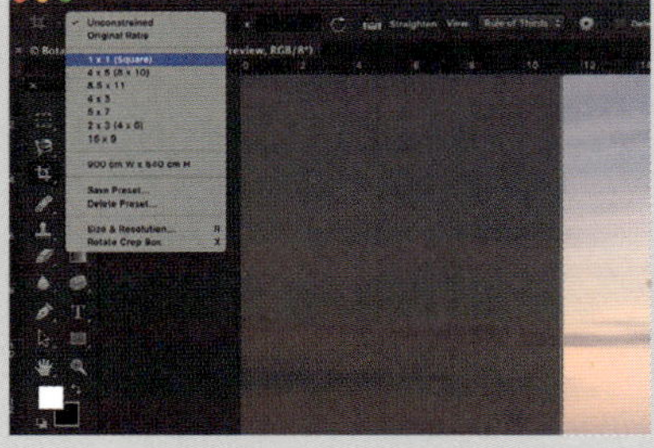

4 You can create a custom crop by entering the values you desire in the width and height boxes. Once done, click Enter or Return to apply your crop.

5 Select five landscape images and crop each three times—into a 1:1 square, 3:1 panoramic, and also 4:3. Which format do you think works best on each, and why? Use the grid opposite to record your findings.

IMAGE 1	
1:1	
3:1	
4:3	
IMAGE 2	
1:1	
3:1	
4:3	
IMAGE 3	
1:1	
3:1	
4:3	
IMAGE 4	
1:1	
3:1	
4:3	
IMAGE 5	
1:1	
3:1	
4:3	

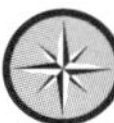

SPECIAL KIT

- Short telephoto lens (60–100mm)

TIPS

- Woodland is a good place to look for miniature landscapes, as is the coast.

- One drawback of using longer focal lengths is the limited depth of field they provide, so opt for a small aperture or consider focus-stacking (see page 35).

FIELD NOTES

- Low-contrast light often suits this style of photography. As you don't need great light or blazing skies this is a good assignment for a gray day.

- Compositions are typically less obvious and harder to identify—don't expect them to jump out at you.

GET CLOSE

Photographing the "intimate landscape" typically involves isolating just a few, select elements, rather than capturing an extensive view. This gives you the freedom to be less conventional and more creative. For this assignment, swap your wideangle lens for a short telephoto, and look closely for detail, texture, structure, shape, or form.

Keep your compositions concise and simple. Aim to bring one or two elements together in an interesting way. Consider excluding the sky from the frame in order to make the landscape less familiar and to distort scale—make the viewer's imagination do some work. Need some inspiration? Look up the work of photographers such as Eliot Porter, Hans Strand, and Guy Tal.

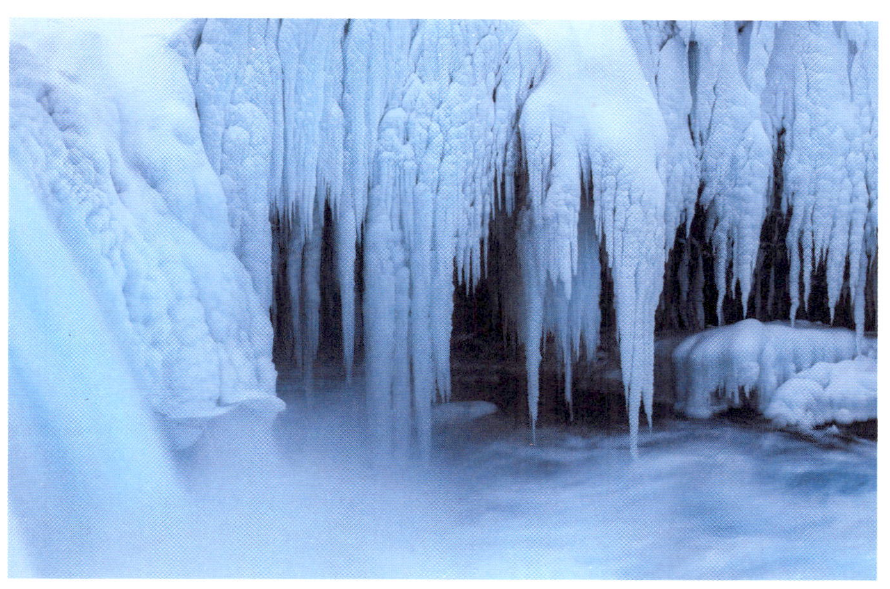

▲ *Look for repetitions, patterns, colors, and contrasts in the landscape.*

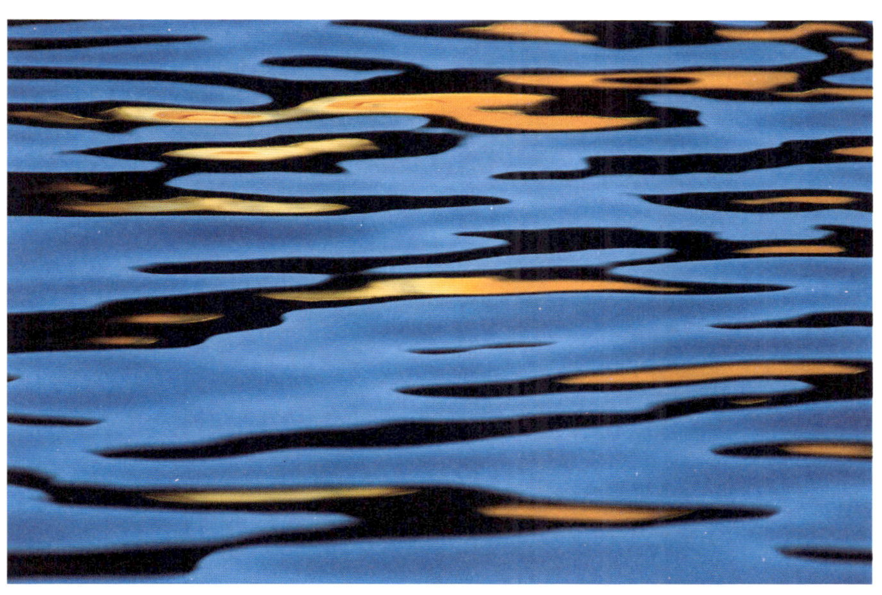

▲ *Highlighting just a small part of the scene can convey more about the landscape than a broader view.*

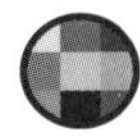

TIPS

- Think outside the box. Itten's list (see main text) is not exhaustive and should be used as a starting point for your own inspiration. Try to think of more conceptual or non-visual contrasts, such as loud/quiet.

CAPTURE CONTRASTS

This assignment takes us back to one of the building blocks of composition: contrast. The importance of contrast was emphasized by the Bauhaus school of art, design, and architecture. The design instructor Johannes Itten felt that contrast was the basis for composition and he produced a list of contrasts, which included these pairs: large/small, hard/soft, thick/thin, light/heavy, straight/curved, continuous/intermittent, much/little, pointed/blunt, light/dark, loud/soft, black/white, strong/weak, diagonal/ circular. While few designs make use of just one kind of contrast, one type usually does dominate the others.

Set yourself a time limit of 2–3 hours, visit a location, and, using the list above as inspiration, shoot as many pictures illustrating different types of contrasts as you can.

FIELD NOTES

Time for observing and thinking is important in this assignment. Resist the temptation to get your camera out immediately, and instead spend some time walking around, looking for different types of contrasts. Having found some, spend some time thinking about how they could be used as the basis for compositions. When you are ready, start shooting.

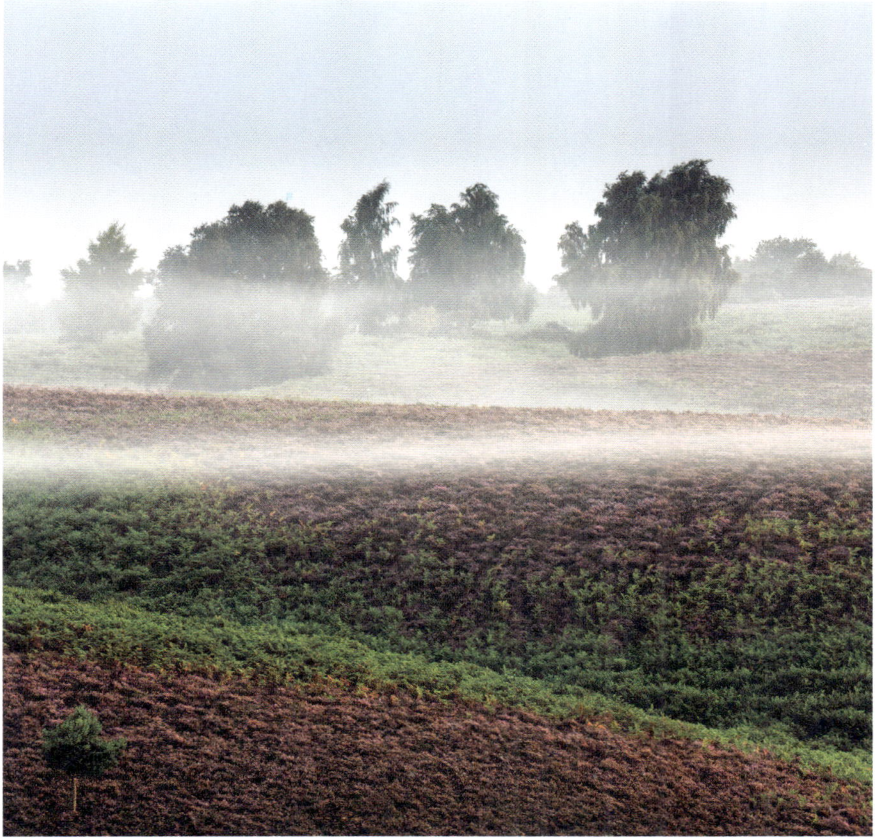

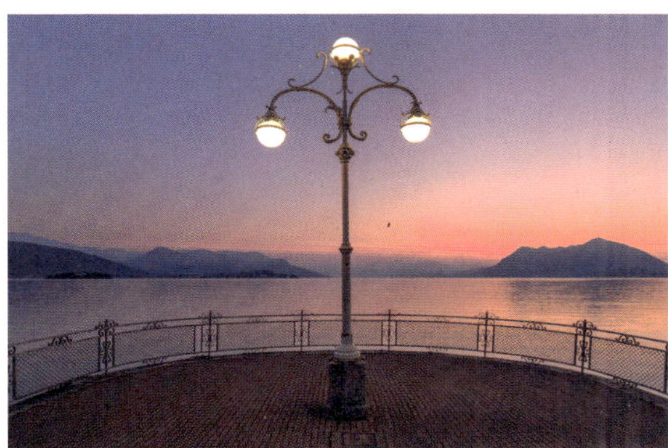

▲ I found myself drawn to this composition, without really wondering why—probably because of the combination of the symmetry and the contrast of straight and curved lines.

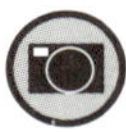

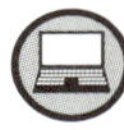

GETTING LEVEL

Getting the tripod and camera completely level is the key to a good panorama. Use a tripod with a built-in spirit level to help you set up accurately—a leveling base (purchased separately from your tripod) will make this even easier. Use your camera's electronic level if it has one or use a hotshoe-mounted bubble level. A pan-and-tilt tripod head or a three-way geared head will make it easier to get your camera level.

SPECIAL KIT

- Tripod (with spirit level)

- Stable tripod head

- Leveling base (optional)

- Post-processing software, such as Adobe Photoshop or Lightroom

TIPS

- Shoot in Manual exposure mode, so the exposure is consistent across the frames.

- Allow extra space at the top and bottom of the image for cropping.

- Don't use a polarizing filter. As the camera angle changes, so will the amount of polarization, which will be uneven across the frames as a result.

- Pan the camera between each shot, allowing an overlap of around 30 per cent from one shot to the next.

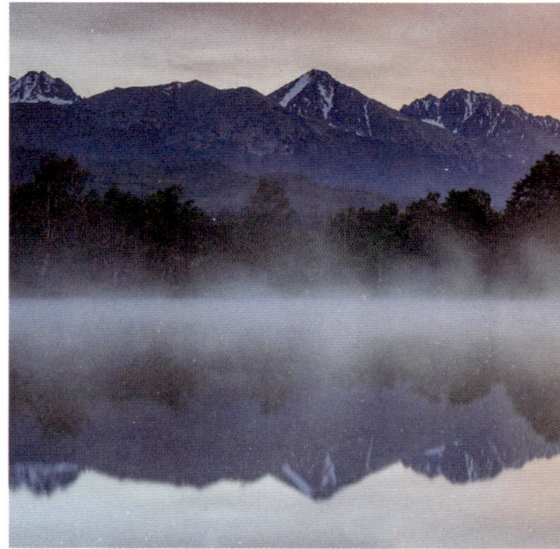

CREATE A PANORAMA

Panoramic images have an enduring appeal, mainly because they most closely replicate our viewing experience when we look at a big vista: our eyes scan across the scene, taking it all in. The adoption of the widescreen format as standard for TV and movies has arguably boosted their popularity further in recent years.

Creating a stitched panorama is a two-stage process. First, you need to take a series of shots, then you need to combine them into a single panoramic image on the computer. Specialist software is available to "stitch" images together, but excellent results can be obtained using the industry standard software, Adobe Lightroom or Photoshop. Photoshop Elements also has the facility to merge images. Specialist tripod heads for shooting panoramas are available—these make lining up your shots easier—but, unless you plan on creating a lot of them, any good, stable head will do.

Serious panorama photographers will insist that images should be shot in portrait (vertical) format, which means you will need to shoot seven or more images to provide a wide enough view. It's certainly true that you will get less distortion if you stitch vertical images, but for this assignment you can shoot in landscape orientation and post-process using the instructions overleaf. As long as you have no close foreground, you won't run into any serious problems. This also has the advantage of requiring fewer images, and therefore there is less chance of the light changing dramatically in the time it takes to shoot your sequence.

▼ *Scenes with reflections are a natural choice for panoramas, especially if there is plenty of interest stretching across the background.*

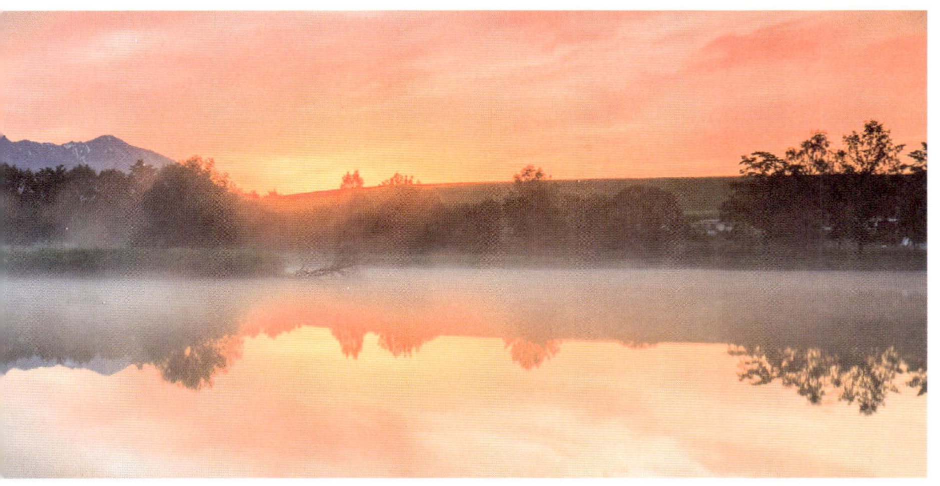

THE PROCESS

To post-process the images, follow the step-by-step tutorial. We have used Lightroom, but you could also use Photoshop or Photoshop Elements.

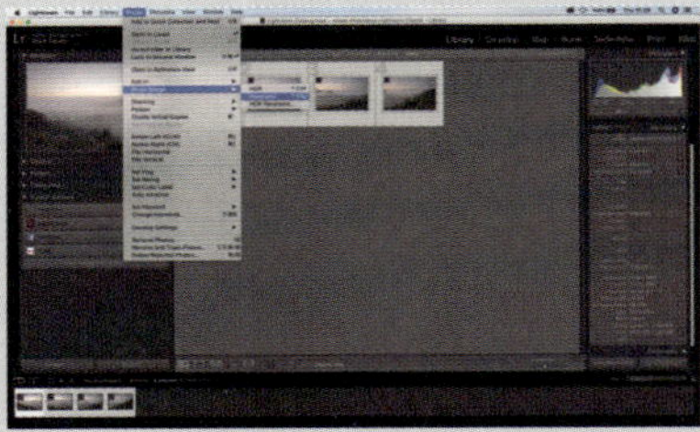

1 Import your images and, in the Library module, select the ones you want to stitch—but don't process any of them yet. Go to Photo > Photomerge > Panorama.

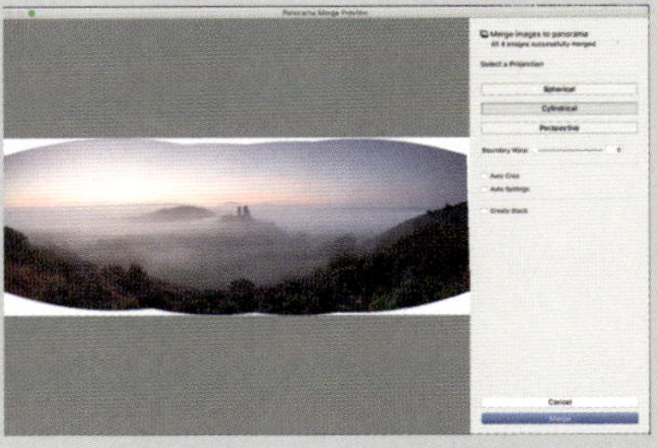

2 You will see the Panorama Merge Preview dialog box. You can choose from three projections: Spherical, Cylindrical, and Perspective. Experiment to see which looks best. In this example, Cylindrical gives the best result.

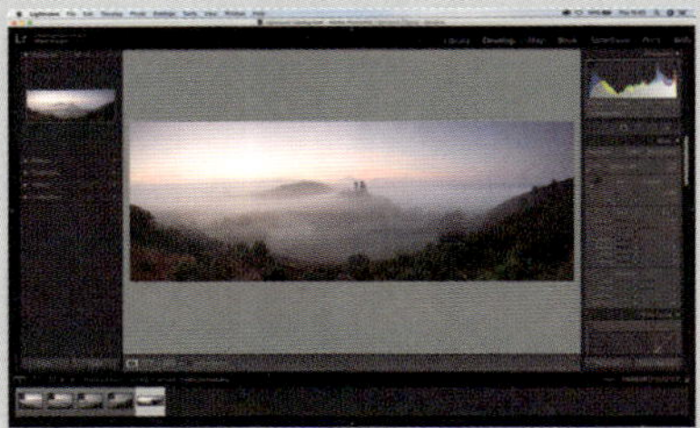

5 Click Merge. Lightroom creates a DNG file, which you can then process as you would any other, using Lightroom's tone controls. Doing this manually at this stage will give better results than clicking Auto Settings in the Photomerge dialog box.

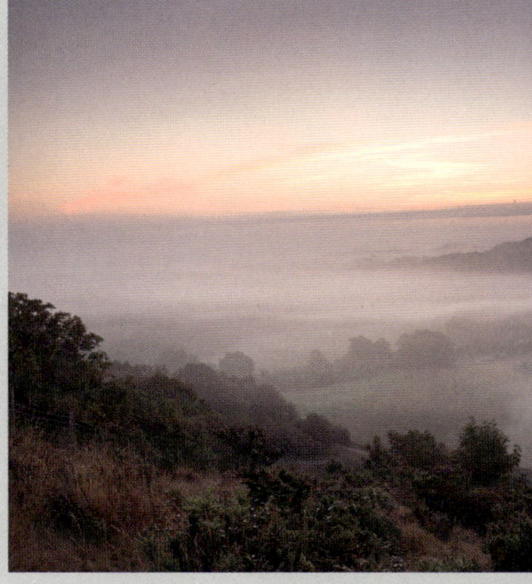

6 The final, post-processed image is stitched together from four horizontal images.

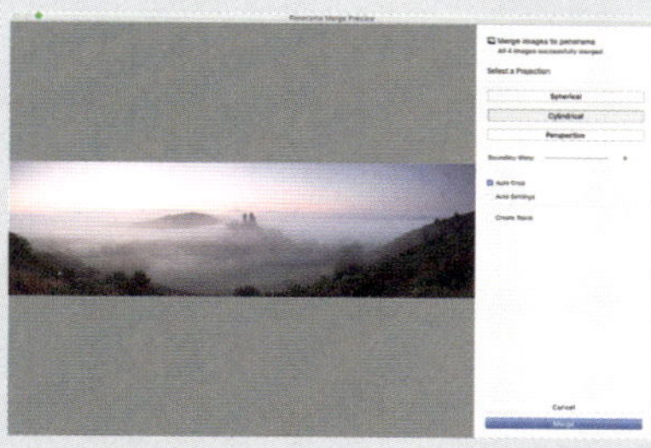 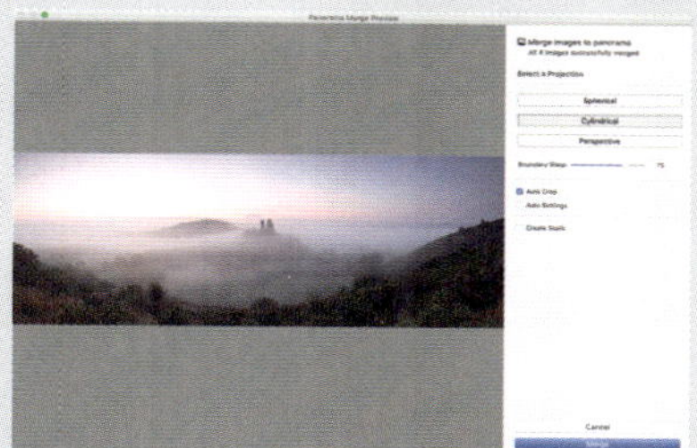

3 Select Auto Crop to remove undesired transparent areas around the edges of the image.

4 Use the Boundary Warp slider to warp the image to fill the canvas. This allows you to preserve parts of the image on the edges of the frame that may otherwise be lost when cropping.

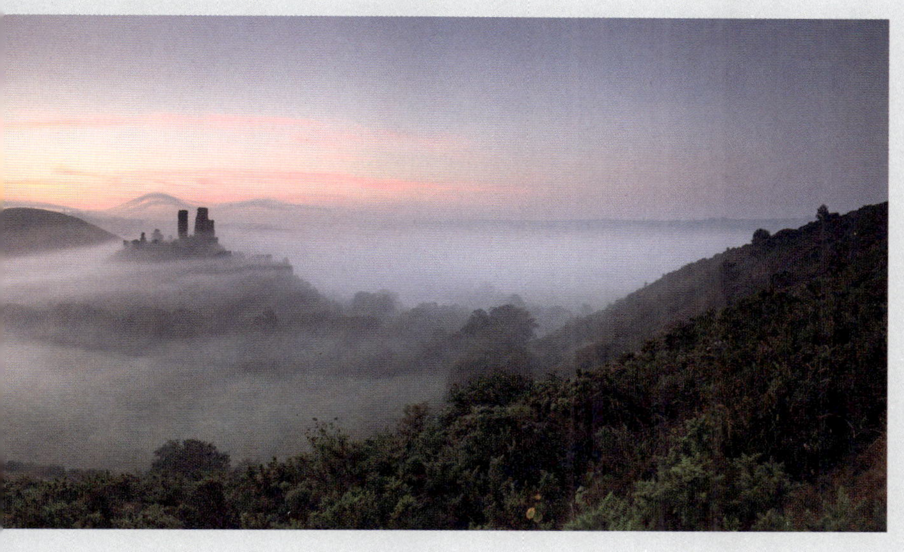

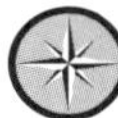

SPECIAL KIT

- Tripod

- Neutral density (ND) filters

- Polarizing filter

- Rain cover

- Chamois leather or microfiber cloth

TIPS

- With waves, timing is important—you can either shoot them as they break and run up the shore or as they drag back out to sea. The latter can create very attractive trails.

- If you change shutter speeds, you will also need to change other values to ensure the correct exposure, such as using a stronger or weaker neutral density filter, or adjusting ISO, for instance.

- A polarizing filter can remove surface glare and make the water look darker—this can enhance an image and increase the contrast between dark and white water.

- Getting close to the water will make the effect of motion more obvious, but take care as water and cameras do not mix!

FIELD NOTES

It's not possible to say exactly which shutter speed will give the best results, as so much depends on the amount of water and how quickly it's moving. Generally speaking, though, moderate-sized waves look good with shutter speeds of 4 or 5 sec. and waterfalls and fast-flowing rivers need a shorter exposure of around 2 sec. However, when on location, you'll need to experiment with different shutter speeds and review your images on the camera's LCD screen to see which gives the best effect.

GO WITH THE FLOW

There is something about the rush of water that is both beautiful and exciting. Many of us could probably spend hours simply gazing at crashing waves or tumbling waterfalls. The challenge with stills photography is how to convey a sense of motion in a single frame. The trend in recent years has been to use extreme ND filters to blur water to a silky texture, creating a calm, tranquil look. Although the results can be beautiful, they do not necessarily convey a sense of movement in the water.

The aim of this assignment is to photograph moving water in a way that captures a sense of motion. Few of us live very far from water, so whether it's the sea, a waterfall, a cascading river, or a stream, there's sure to be a suitable subject fairly close by.

To convey the feeling of moving water, you really need to avoid the extreme shutter speeds—neither freezing water droplets in mid-air with a 1/1000 sec. exposure, nor blurring water so that it looks like mist. The best results are obtained with shutter speeds that retain some texture in the water—the exact speed will vary, depending on the speed of flow and amount of water. Experiment and select half a dozen shots that meet the brief.

▼ *An exposure of 4 sec. has helped retain texture in the waves. Shooting as the wave dragged back out to sea has created trails across the rocky ledge in the foreground.*

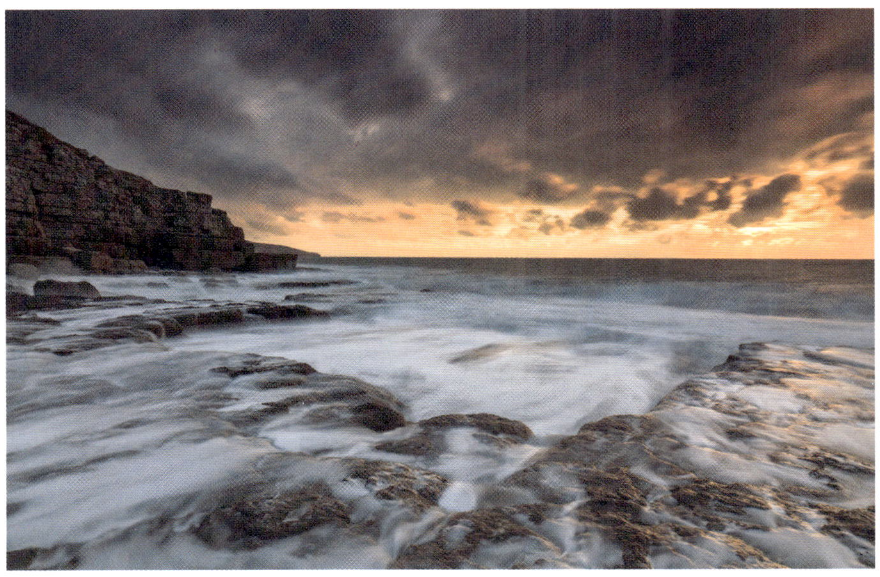

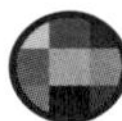

TIPS

- The best time of day to shoot silhouettes is when the sun is low above the horizon and the sky is bright, close to sunrise and sunset.

- Look for instantly recognizable subjects to silhouette, such as a skeletal tree, building, or well-known landmark.

- Use your camera's Live View histogram to guide you. When shooting silhouettes, expect your histogram to be skewed to the left of the graph. While this would normally indicate incorrect exposure, in this case, underexposure is intentional and creative.

- Remove graduated neutral density (ND) filters—for this type of image, you don't want to record detail in the landscape.

SHOOT AGAINST THE LIGHT

A correct exposure is really one that records a scene or subject in the way the photographer intended. Once you have fully mastered exposure, you can then manipulate it creatively. One way to do this is to use exposure to create a silhouette of your subject, by using an extreme form of "contre jour," or "against the light" photography, with the subject strongly backlit and recorded as a black outline, devoid of color or detail. Combined with just the right subject matter, the results can be dramatic and eye-catching.

Anything between your camera and the sun, or the surrounding sky, can appear as a dark shape. It is important you expose for the brighter sky and not for the darker foreground, so spot meter for a bright area of the sky. The exposure will be correct for the sky, but grossly underexposed for foreground subjects, creating a silhouette.

Knowing how to create a silhouette is just part of the equation, though, as your subject choice and shooting angle will make or break your contre jour shots. Given that your subject will be devoid of color or detail, it is important to photograph a

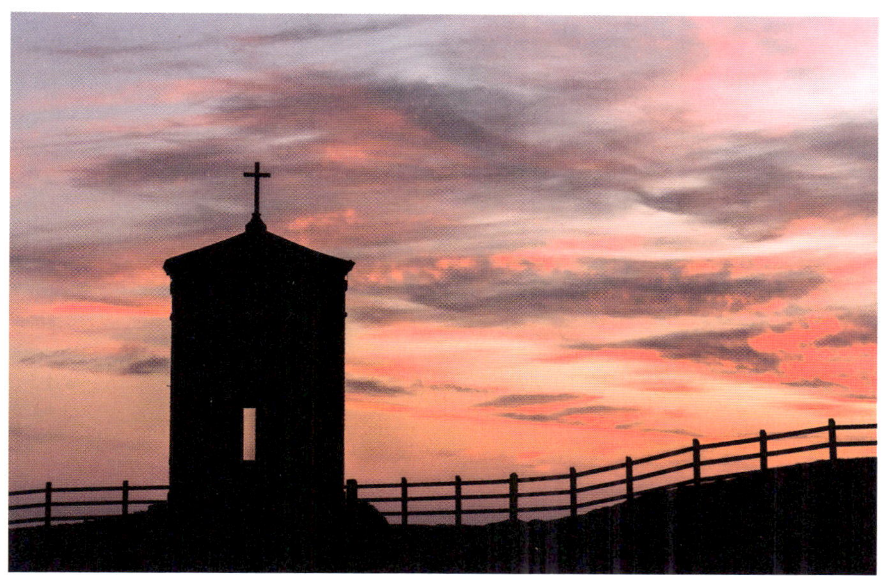

▲ *A colorful or dramatic sky will create an ideal backdrop for a silhouetted subject.*

scene or subject with a strong and recognizable outline, such as a tree, building, or landmark. Select a perspective where you can isolate your subject and project it clearly against a brighter backdrop, and be careful not to include anything that distracts from your subject—simplicity often works best. Also, avoid overlapping your subject with other objects, as this will severely reduce the impact of the image.

FIELD NOTES

To cast your subject into silhouette, meter for the brighter sky using spot metering mode, available on most DSLRs and mirrorless cameras. This mode reads light from just a small proportion of the image space—typically two or three per cent. By aiming the spot-metering point at a bright area of the sky, the camera will bias settings for this area. Consequently, the darker foreground will be underexposed and rendered as silhouette.

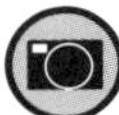
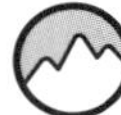

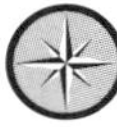

TIPS

- You may need to increase ISO to generate a shutter speed fast enough to eliminate camera shake. High ISO performance is now so good that noise should be well controlled, even at ISO 1600.

- Consider switching on Auto ISO. You can manually set or limit the ISO range to ensure speeds don't stray too high. We recommend setting a range of ISO 100–1000. The camera will automatically adjust the ISO to help maintain a usable handheld shutter speed.

- When shooting without a tripod, avoid using filters that prolong exposure, such as solid neutral density (ND) or polarizing filters.

SHOOT HANDHELD

As a landscape enthusiast there is an assumption that you should always use a tripod, and for most of the assignments in this book a tripod will either be helpful or essential. However, you don't always need a camera support and—on occasion—the speed and spontaneity of shooting handheld will be a more practical and creative choice. Tripods can hinder your movement and anchor you to one spot, and to find the best shooting angle and perspective you often need to move about. So, for this assignment, leave your tripod at home and explore the possibilities of handheld.

Shooting handheld for even a few hours will remind you to explore and be creative. Although being tripod-free will prevent you from shooting in extreme low light and using lengthy exposures, there are plenty of subjects it suits. It can also encourage you to explore awkward or unconventional angles. For example, achieving unusually low or high perspectives is easier without a support, and techniques like intentional camera movement (see page 114) lend themselves to handheld photography. If you regularly use a tripod, you will find the experience of shooting handheld—and being able to quickly and instinctively alter your composition—quite liberating.

It is always a good idea to compose your images slightly more loosely than you would normally, to allow for any slight camera movement when you press the shutter. You can then tidy up the composition using the Crop Tool during post-processing.

When shooting handheld, always be mindful of what your shutter speed is doing. The risk of camera shake is enhanced and you should avoid shooting in low light. However, with active image stabilization and good technique, you will be able to shoot at speeds as low as 1/60 sec. with a wideangle lens. Remember to review image sharpness regularly.

FIELD NOTES

- Switch on image stabilization on your camera or lens—this will allow you to shoot handheld at slower shutter speeds without camera shake.

- To keep your camera stable, stand with your feet roughly shoulder-width apart, with one foot slightly in front of the other. Keep your elbows tucked in toward your chest and try to hold the camera firmly to your face.

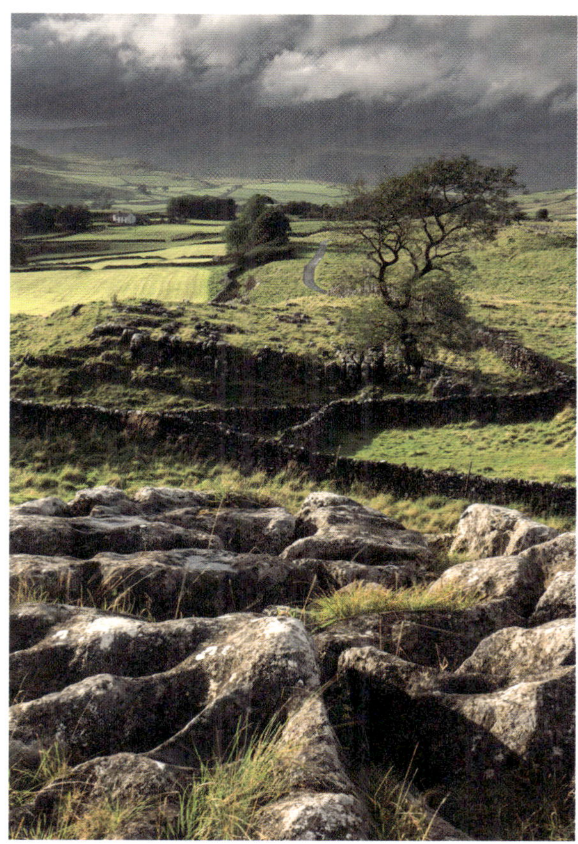

▲ *A tripod is an essential tool in many assignments, but purposefully working without one can be liberating, and encourage a spontaneous reaction to transient light.*

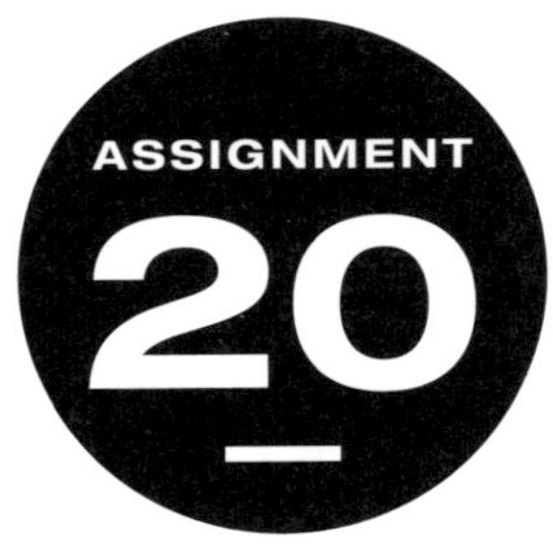

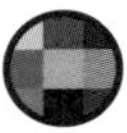

TIPS

- If you shoot images in Raw format, you can quickly and precisely adjust White Balance during post-processing. However, if you capture JPEGs, it is more important to get the White Balance the way you want it in-camera.

FIND BALANCE

You will probably already be familiar with the White Balance (WB) button on your camera, but do you know what it actually does? For this assignment, you will learn its role and discover that it is a function you can also use creatively.

White Balance is designed to neutralize color casts produced by various light sources. Cameras are programmed with a choice of presets to mimic common light types, such as Daylight, Cloudy, Shade, and Incandescent lighting, for instance. However, the camera's Auto WB setting will normally do a great job of recording the light's temperature faithfully, and this is the setting you are normally recommended to use. But whoever said you have to record the light's color faithfully? You can also use White Balance to artificially warm up or cool down a scene, and so influence the mood of the image. Here's your chance to try it for yourself...

Take a series of shots of the same image using each one of your camera's various WB preset values. Compare the results side-by-side. You will see the Cloudy and Shade settings make the scene warmer—perfect for enhancing a sunset or fall color. In contrast, the Tungsten and Incandescent presets will cool down the image with an icy-blue hue. Once you understand its role, you can deliberately mismatch White Balance to create color casts for added drama and visual impact.

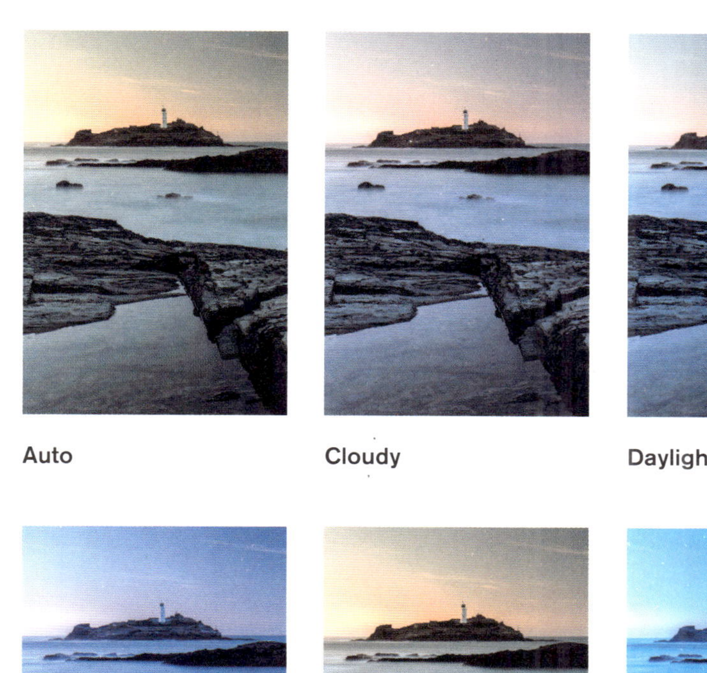

Auto | Cloudy | Daylight

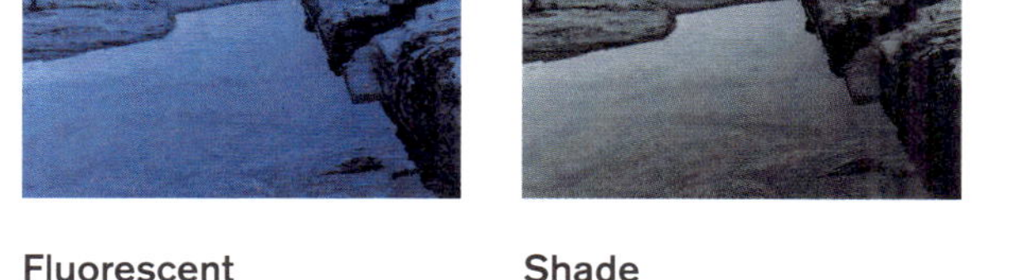

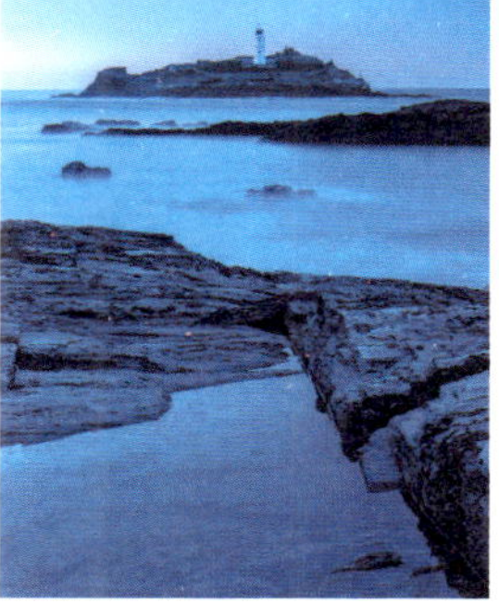

Fluorescent | Shade | Tungsten

▲ *The most aesthetically pleasing color temperature will not always be the technically correct one! Have fun playing with your camera's White Balance until you find the effect you like.*

FIELD NOTES

In addition to the camera's WB presets, you can dial in your own custom Kelvin value, or color temperature. This ranges typically between 2,500 and 10,000K, but depends on the camera model—the higher the value, the warmer the resulting image will appear.

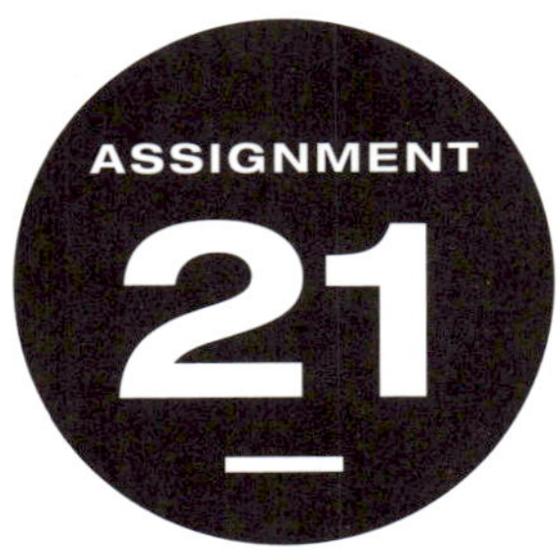

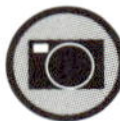

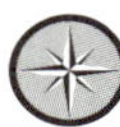

TIPS

- Placing the subject centrally is discouraged, but there are occasions when it works well—for instance, when there are strong lines "funneling" attention toward the subject, and in minimalist compositions with a lot of negative space around the subject.

- Reflections often look better when symmetry is employed in the composition, rather than dividing the frame more conventionally according to the design theory called the Rule of Thirds.

- The square format naturally suits bold, graphic compositions with a central subject.

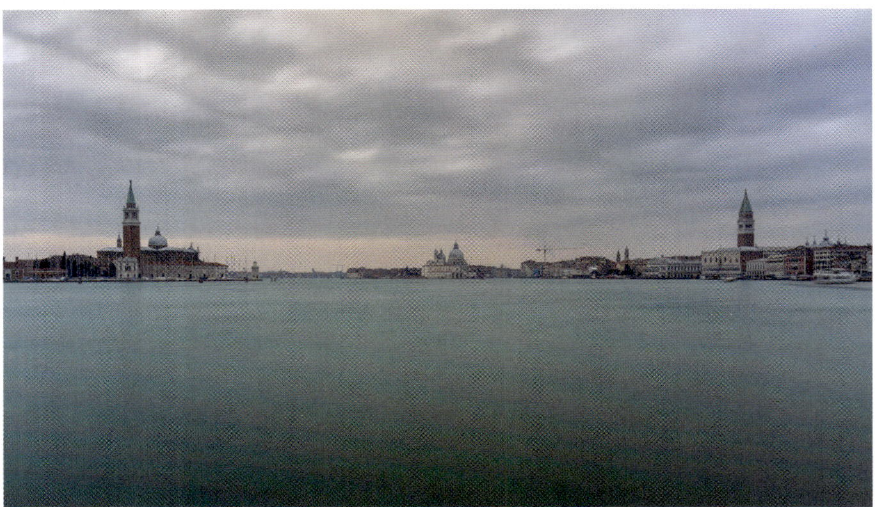

BREAK THE RULES

Rules abound in landscape photography and they are designed to help us create balanced compositions and achieve technical accuracy. Some of the better known include: the Rule of Thirds, which determines the placement of key compositional elements, such as the focal point and the horizon, by visualizing a grid of nine squares; the Golden Section, which divides up the frame according to a particularly harmonious ratio found in nature; and the Rule of Odds, which suggests that an odd number of subjects is inherently more interesting than an even number. Other common tendencies in landscape photography are extreme depth of field, filling foregrounds with a suitable subject, and an unwillingness to place the main subject at the center of the frame.

Knowing the rules is obviously important. Slavishly following a set of guidelines, however, can result in images that are rather stale and "samey." It can be fun, inspiring, and sometimes necessary to break the rules. For this assignment, set your imagination free, follow your instinct, and deliberately break the design rules to see if you can create something visually exciting.

There is a danger that your images will lack cohesion and structure. But if you work with a critical eye and try to develop a feeling for what works and what doesn't, you should be able to create a selection of strikingly different photographs.

◄ This image breaks many rules: it was shot in the "unphotogenic" middle of the day, there is no foreground interest, the horizon is central, and there are two strong focal points toward the edges of the frame, competing for attention. However, its symmetry appeals and the tension created by the two towers adds interest. The soft colors of overcast daylight complement the scene and the semi-panoramic crop reduces the impact of the empty foreground.

FIELD NOTES

If there is a particularly strong sky, don't be afraid to abandon the Rule of Thirds and let the sky dominate the frame.

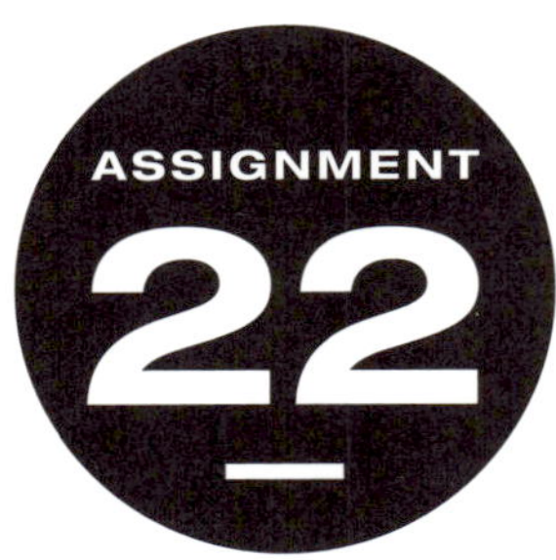

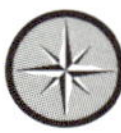

SPECIAL KIT

- 50mm prime lens, or a standard zoom lens set at 50mm

TIPS

- Prime 50mm lenses tend to have a fast maximum aperture, in the region of f/1.4–f/1.8. This lets you play with differential focus, using a large aperture to throw parts of the landscape creatively out of focus.

- Prime lenses tend to be bitingly sharp. A prime 35mm or 50mm lens can be a good choice when you wish to create a stitched panorama (see page 44).

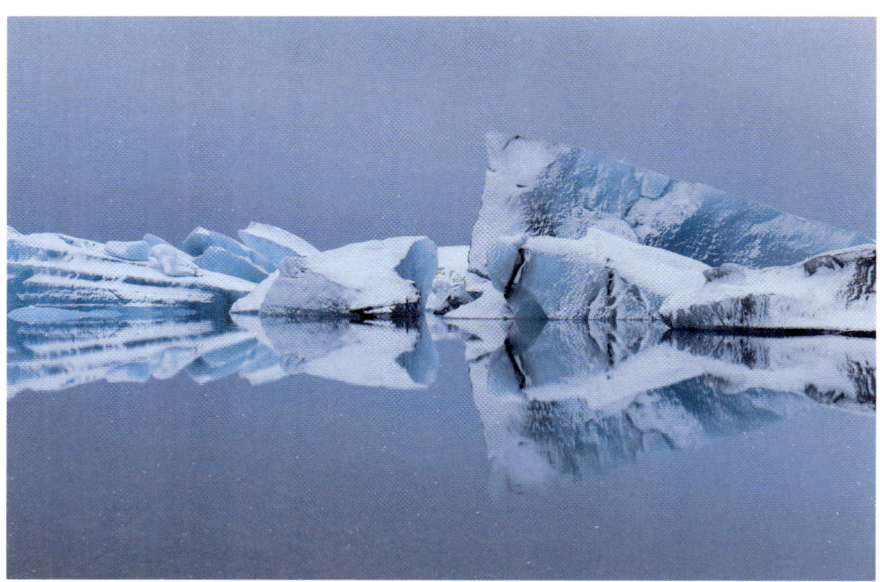

NIFTY FIFTY

Unsurprisingly, zoom lenses are popular today and their versatility means they are the mainstay of many photographers' kit bags. However, zooms can also make photographers lazy when composing shots and it is important to learn when it is better to physically move the camera in order to create the best perspective or shooting angle. For this challenge, you will need to use a fixed focal length lens for a day and learn the benefits of zooming with your feet.

Using just one, fixed focal length will help you develop your composition skills, forcing you to be more careful, accurate, and disciplined. It will also make you think more about your positioning and framing.

You can use any fixed focal length for this challenge, but we recommend using a 50mm prime lens. A 50mm lens offers a similar angle of view to the human eye so it provides a fairly natural-looking perspective. So-called "standard" or "nifty fifty" lenses are typically inexpensive to buy, have a fast maximum aperture, and are optically superb. But if you don't own one—and don't have the inclination or budget to rush out and buy one—you can simply set your zoom lens at 50mm for the day. Now see what you can capture!

Just carrying one lens will make your camera bag light and encourage you to walk further and explore new viewpoints. You will need to think much harder about exactly where you set up and your shooting angle. By having to work harder to create successful compositions you will become a better, more imaginative, and more adaptable landscape photographer.

◄ *A standard 50mm lens length will help you fix focus on key elements and isolate interest within the landscape.*

FIELD NOTES

This assignment might seem limiting at first, but using just one focal length will force you to move around the landscape more to find the best angle, distance, and perspective. Try working handheld (see page 52) to give you extra freedom of movement.

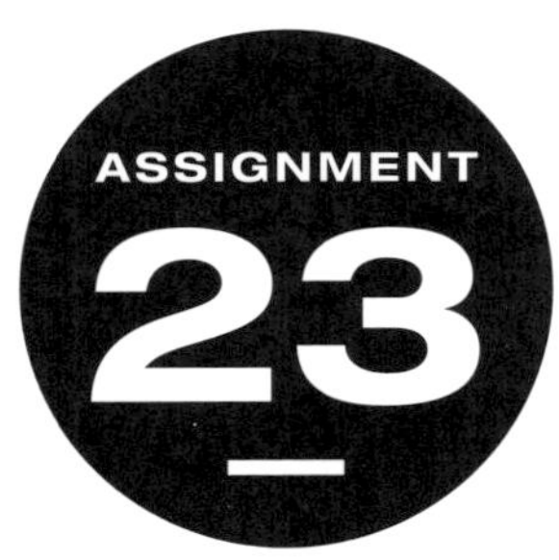

SPECIAL KIT

- A telephoto zoom lens

TIPS

- Telephoto lenses have a reputation for being heavy and expensive. However, only fast optics (with a large maximum aperture of f/2.8 or f/4) are really costly. A standard telephoto zoom lens in the range 70–300mm is usually an affordable and a useful lens to add to your system.

GO LONG

Due to their stretched perspective, wideangle lenses are the obvious choice for photographing landscapes. But it is not healthy for your photography to grow over-reliant on any one lens. Therefore, for this assignment, you must only use a focal length of 200mm or longer.

By the end of this assignment, you will better understand how focal length influences the way you capture the landscape. Telephoto lengths appear to foreshorten perspective and help place emphasis on distant objects and interest, such as rolling hills, mountain peaks, or far-away buildings. A longer lens will allow you to exclude unnecessary elements from the frame and simplify chaotic-looking landscapes. Compression will create a "stacked" or "layering" effect—where objects in the landscape appear pushed up closer to one another.

Using a telephoto lens will increase your versatility and creative options. And once you've completed this long lens assignment, you will consider one an integral part of your landscape kit!

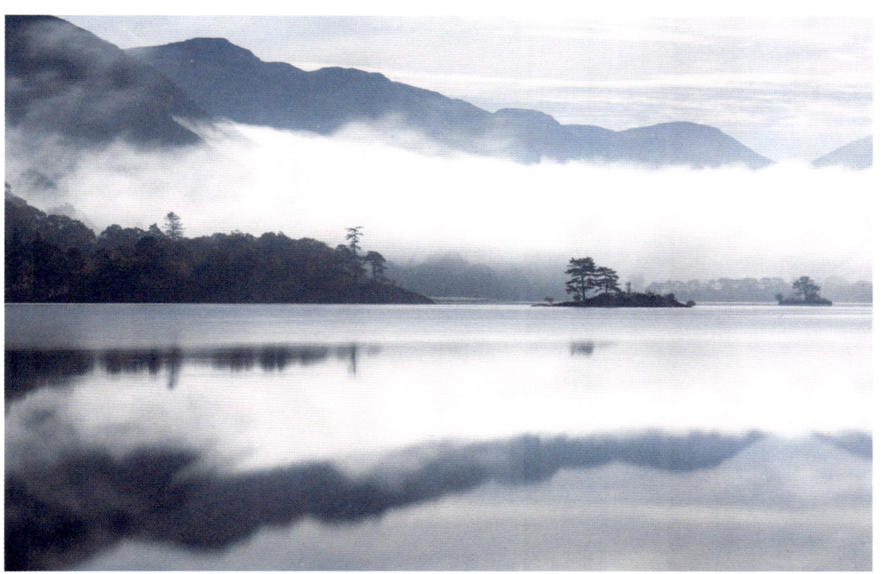

▲ *A telephoto lens will enable you to obscure foregrounds that lack interest, or boring skies. They are also useful for exaggerating the atmospheric effects of weather—for example, mist or snow.*

FIELD NOTES

- Perspective is simply an effect of camera-to-subject distance: the further you are from your subject, the smaller the gap appears between it and its background. Therefore, long lenses do not actually compress perspective, they just create this impression.

- Due to their larger size, longer lenses are more prone to being caught by the wind. Check image sharpness regularly and select a faster shutter speed if needed.

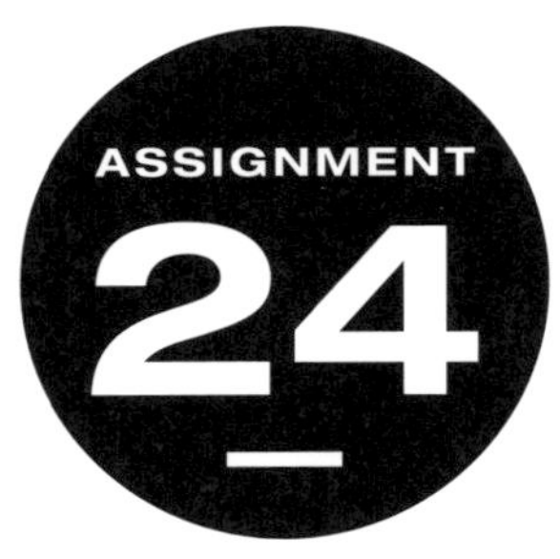

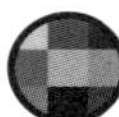
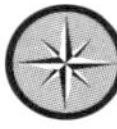
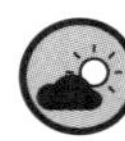

SPECIAL KIT

- Smartphone apps for plotting GPS coordinates and the sun's position, such as SunScout and PhotoPills

TIPS

- To help you compose each image as identically as possible, make a record of the focal length you used for the original. Keep a copy of the photo on your phone (or tablet) to use as a handy reference for when you return and set up again.

FIELD NOTES

- When photographing the same scene at different times of the day, use a sun compass smartphone app (such as SunScout) to calculate the sun's path from morning to evening. This will help decide the best place to set up.

- You can capture GPS coordinates with a smartphone on your first visit and return to the exact same spot.

RETURN TO THE SCENE

No two photographs are exactly the same. You can stand in the same place, use the same camera set-up, and compose your image identically, but the result will still be different. The landscape is constantly changing. Each season will transform the landscape, while the time of day, light, and weather will dictate the mood. Your brief for this assignment is to photograph the same view at different times for an entire year, to capture how that view changes with each of the four seasons.

First, you need to identify a suitable scene to photograph. For convenience, opt for a view close to home that you can visit easily and regularly. Ideally, choose a scene containing trees and foliage so that seasonal changes will be more obvious. Try to compose your image identically on each visit to help highlight these seasonal differences.

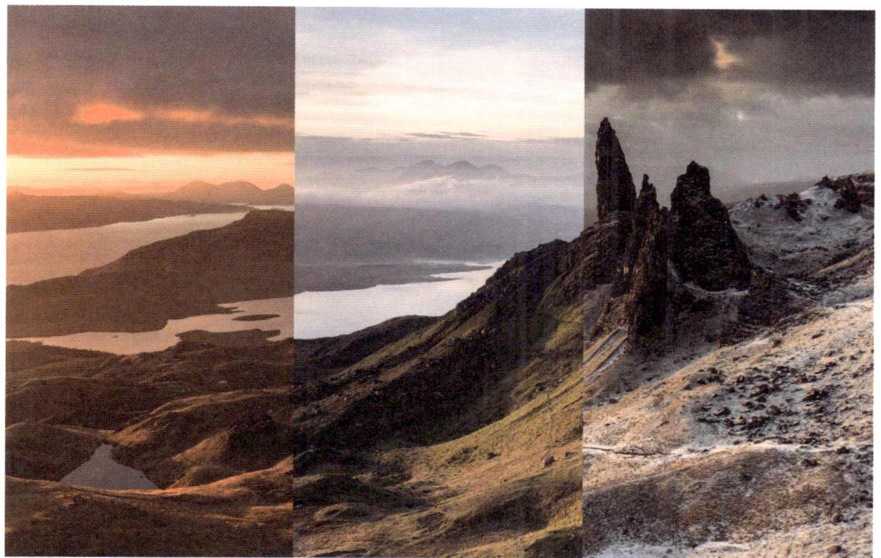

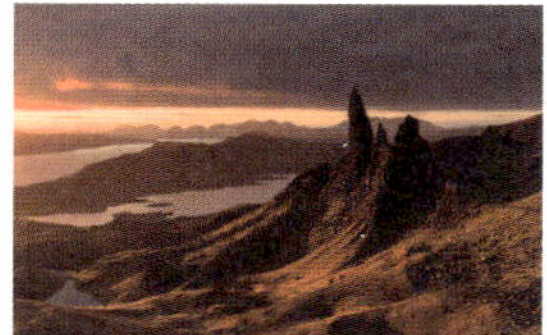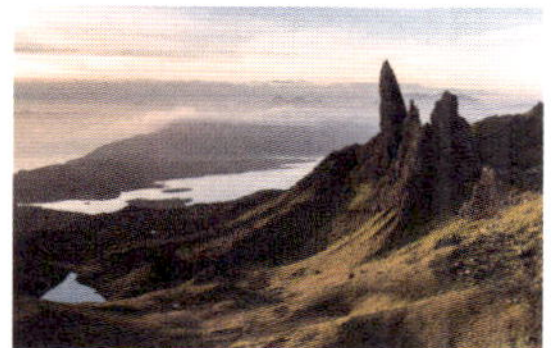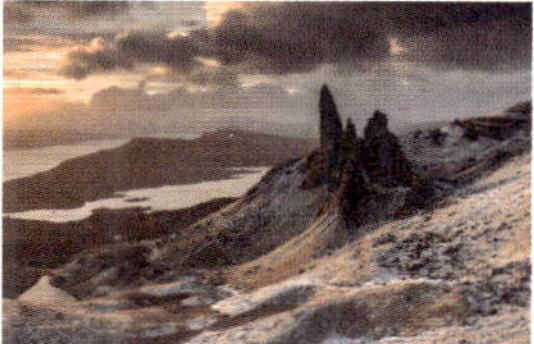

▲ *Returning to the same viewpoint at different times of the year or day will result in an eye-catching sequence of shots.*

If you can't wait twelve months to finish the assignment, simply photograph the same scene at different times of the day—for example, at hourly intervals from sunset to sunset. Maybe even photograph the same scene at night, too. Or shoot in different weather conditions until you build a collection of contrasting shots.

Whichever way you interpret this assignment, it is sure to produce some stunning and richly varied results that illustrate that no two photographs of the same place are ever quite the same. Once you've captured your sequence, don't forget to print the images and frame them together. The result might be four shots capturing the story of nature over four seasons; twelve shots creating a calendar of the characteristic light and weather of the different months; or half a dozen images telling the story of a single day in the life of a landscape.

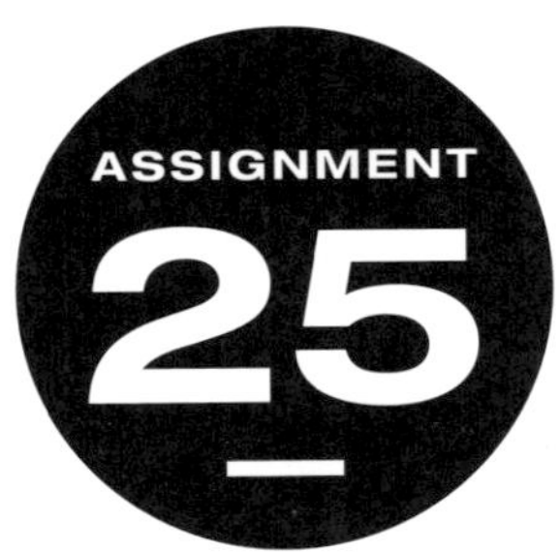

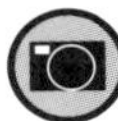

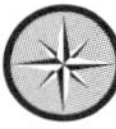

SPECIAL KIT

- Maps

- Compass

TIPS

- No apps or technology are allowed, just good old-fashioned maps and a compass.

- Trust your instincts: use intuition and experience to gauge the weather and conditions.

▶ *There is one exception to the rules given here: if you intend visiting more remote locations, check the weather forecast (and tide times, if applicable) for safety.*

BE SPONTANEOUS

Landscape photographers are encouraged to meticulously plan and prepare. Using a host of apps, they calculate the sun's precise position, view detailed weather graphs, and access up-to-the minute tide charts. Some apps even predict if there is likely to be a colorful sky or not. There is no doubting the usefulness of these apps and websites; they can help you work efficiently and maximize your chances of success. But unless you are careful, they can also make photographs repetitive and predictable, seducing you to return to the same viewpoints in the same combination of conditions. This assignment is intended to make you rely more on chance…

Your brief is to visit somewhere you have never previously been. Travel somewhere new and explore. Be inquisitive. Find out exactly where that unknown path goes, what the view from the top of that faraway hill looks like, or what secrets are held in that little woodland you normally pass by. Visit an unfamiliar place at an unfamiliar time in unknown weather, in search of fresh opportunities. The chances of a successful shoot may be reduced, but you will be much more likely to produce original or innovative work.

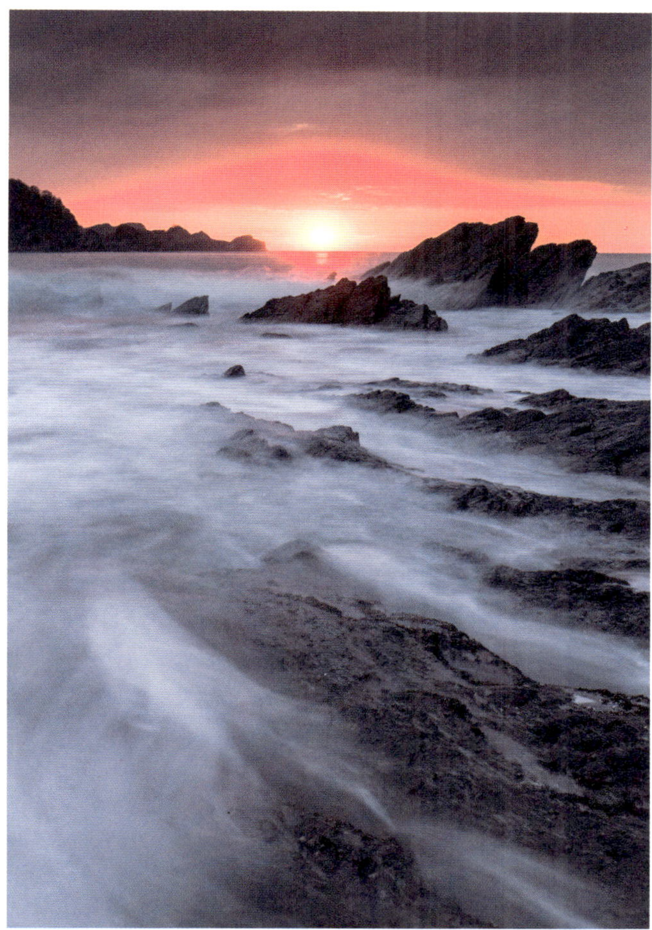

FIELD NOTES

- For this project you will need to rely on your instinct and ability to improvise rather than on your technology.

- Avoid looking at photographs beforehand that might influence your approach or choice of viewpoint. It is easy to subconsciously replicate images you've previously seen and liked.

- This assignment is intended to make you think, enhance your ability to adapt, and most importantly help you produce unique work.

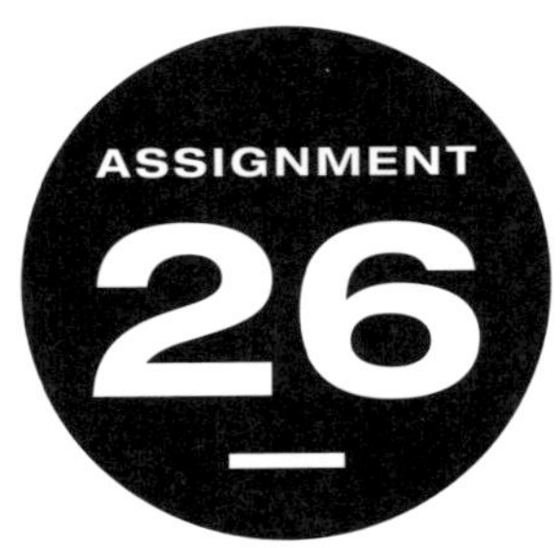

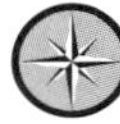

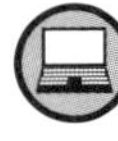

SPECIAL KIT

- Smartphone apps for pinpointing location, day, and time of original image, such as The Photographer's Ephemeris

- Post-processing software, such as Adobe Photoshop or Lightroom

TIPS

- Don't restrict yourself to photographs— you can use a famous landscape painting for inspiration.

- Smartphone apps can be invaluable.

▶ *When planning a trip to Yosemite, I decided to visit Tunnel View, where Ansel Adams had taken many of his famous photographs. I was lucky enough to be there one morning when there was snow in the valley and low cloud was swirling around. The conditions reminded me of Adams' image "Clearing Winter Storm" so I set up a similar composition and converted the image to black and white in post-processing.*

MAKE IT YOUR OWN

There is currently a lot of discussion over the question of originality in landscape photography. With ever-increasing numbers of images being presented online, some feel that there is a tendency for landscape photographers simply to travel from one well-known destination to another, doing little more than copy other people's work.

However, there is value in such an assignment. In all artistic disciplines, copying is a vital part of the learning process, but you can also benefit from the opportunity of studying the working methods and style of a successful photographer by incorporating some elements of these in your own work and learning new skills.

So, use this project as an opportunity to try something new. For example, if you only ever shoot in color, try to recreate a famous monochrome image. This will teach you a lot about composition, structure, and tonality, and may help your personal style to evolve. You can also look beyond the photograph you've chosen: rather than simply

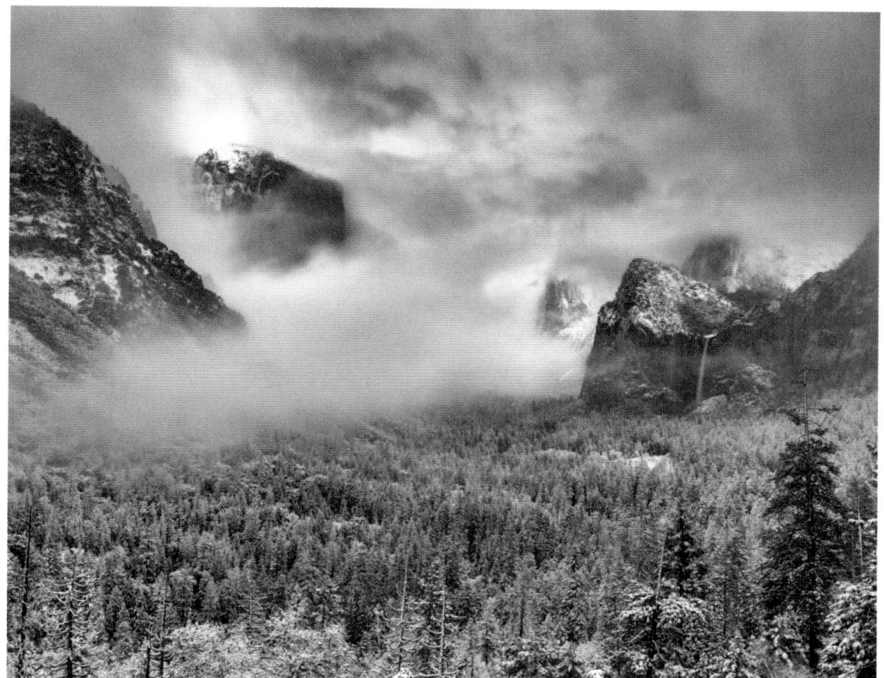

copy it, see if you can add your own twist to the image, perhaps by excluding some elements that were present in the original or adding some that were absent.

Post-processing may be an important part of creating the image. The original may be a black-and-white photograph from the 1950s, for instance, but you are shooting with a DSLR. You will need to research the darkroom techniques used to create the original print and find out how to recreate them digitally.

FIELD NOTES

- Spend time studying your image. Work out where the photographer (or painter) was standing. What time of year and day was it shot and why—does the light only reach this viewpoint in a particular season, for example? Also, find out as much technical information as possible. What camera, lenses, and filters were used? What were the aperture and shutter speed? Are there any particular techniques you think the photographer used, such as maximizing depth of field?

- Although you need to study the original image and be familiar with it, don't take it with you on the shoot—allow for your own interpretation of the scene.

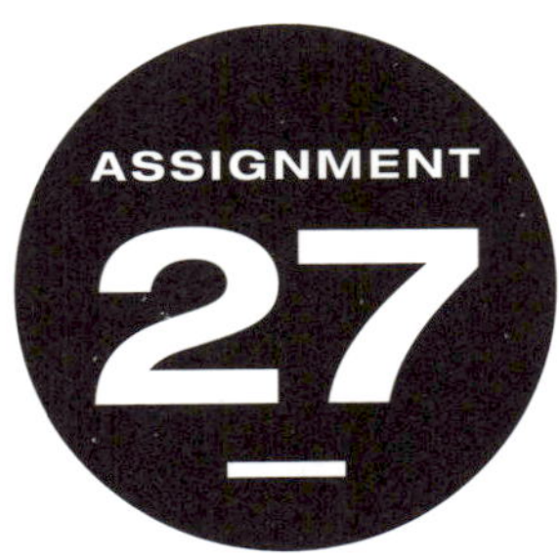

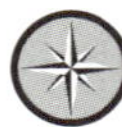

SPECIAL KIT

- Smartphone apps, such as PhotoPills or The Photographer's Ephemeris

TIPS

- Creative photography is not something you should rush. Setting aside time to take photos, without distraction, is key to your development. You will find the experience of going away with your camera liberating, fulfilling, enjoyable, and productive.

- You don't need to take lots of photos for a trip to be considered successful. Always prioritize quality over quantity. Challenge yourself to return with, say, five photographs you are genuinely pleased with. Print your favorite.

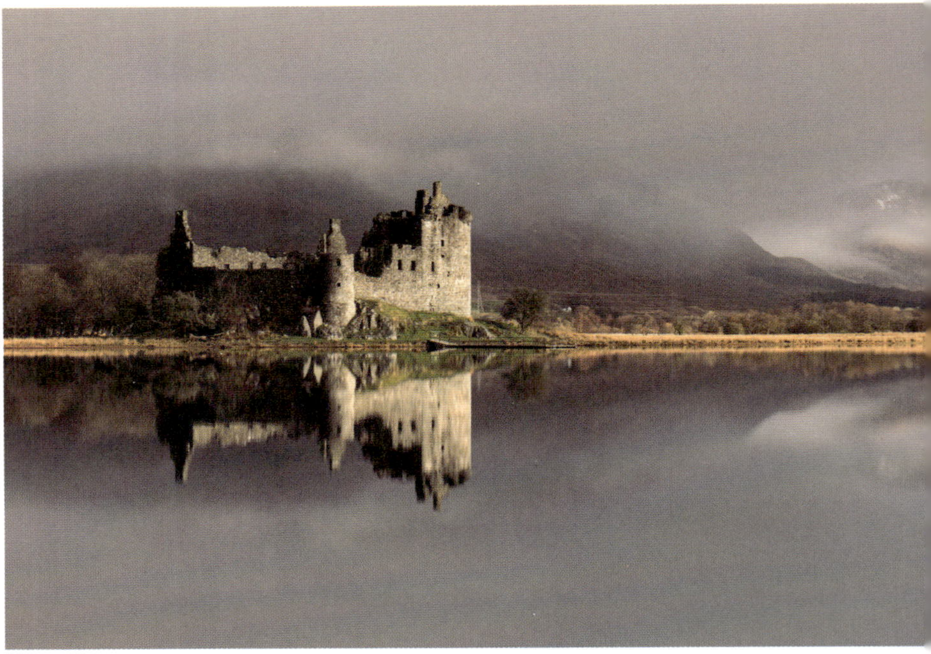

ROAD TRIP

You don't need to invest lots of money in the best photography gear to shoot great landscape images. What you need is opportunity, and one of the best ways to get this is to go on a photography road trip. Revisiting the same places over and over can lead to overfamiliarity and complacency. So, if you suspect staleness in your work, look at a map and begin planning an adventure. Nothing will get your creative juices flowing better than visiting exciting new places, with viewpoints you've never seen before, which you can photograph with fresh eyes.

For this assignment, you don't necessarily have to go far, or be away for more than a day or two—you just need to photograph new places. Much will depend on time and budget. Beforehand, do a little homework on the area you intend visiting. Research potential viewpoints using Google Images or other apps, such as PhotoPills or The Photographer's Ephemeris. This will help you plan where to go and ensure you are efficient with your time. However, avoid simply replicating the most popular shots you see online. The idea of this assignment is to reignite your creativity and innovation—not simply to "collect" new viewpoints. Even if the weather forecast isn't good, you should still go. Adapt to the conditions and persevere. You are sure to return home with some great, fresh images, and some stories to tell.

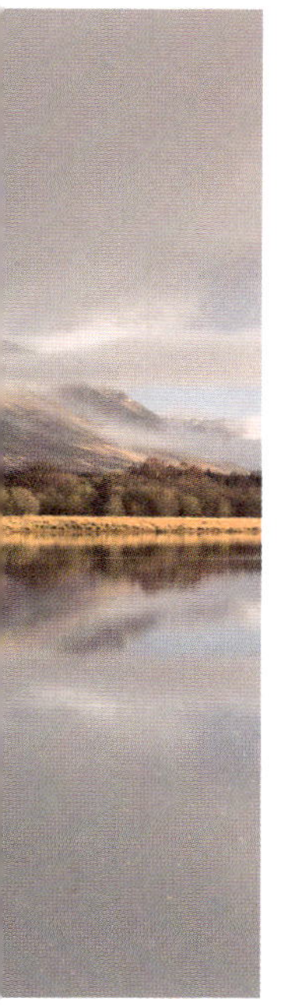

◄ *Visiting new places will reignite your love of the outdoors and photographing the landscape.*

FIELD NOTES

- Camping will allow you to set up close to your dawn location, minimize travel and cost, and maximize sleep! If you don't fancy camping, try a hostel, Airbnb, or guesthouse, or rent a camper van for a couple of days.

- Don't take more kit than you need. Travel light, so you have the freedom to walk further and explore more.

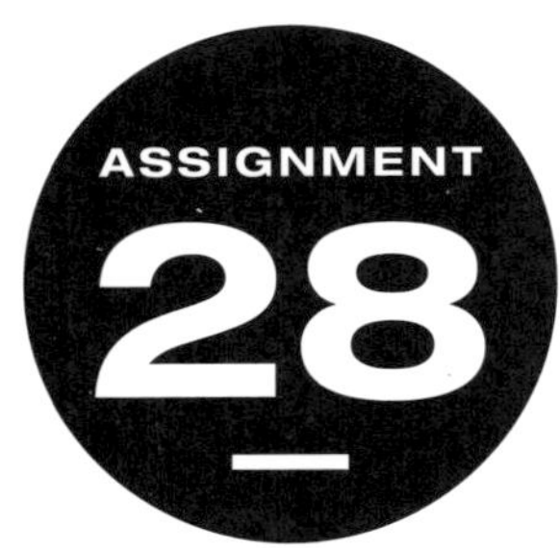

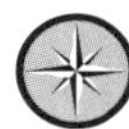

SPECIAL KIT

- Maps

- Smartphone apps, such as PhotoPills or The Photographer's Ephemeris

TIPS

- This is potentially a long-term project. Spend time getting to know the location and be prepared for multiple visits.

- Allow plenty of time for this assignment—research is the key to success here.

GO SOMEWHERE FAMOUS

This is a challenging assignment and one that should really stretch your creativity. If you look at social media and through the pages of photographic magazines, you could be forgiven for thinking that there is a set number of locations and viewpoints to shoot and very specific compositions you have to copy. It is perhaps a valid criticism that there is little new in landscape photography.

One way of creating more original images is, of course, to find locations that have not been photographed before. However, it's not as simple as that. Photography has been around for a while now, it is incredibly popular, and the planet has been thoroughly explored. Famous locations are famous for a reason—with perhaps very few exceptions, they are the most photogenic places you can find. Maybe there are one or two gems still waiting to be discovered, but the odds are against it.

So, rather than trying to be original by shooting inferior locations, we have set a more demanding brief: visit a well-known, well-photographed location and shoot an original picture by finding an alternative to the familiar viewpoints.

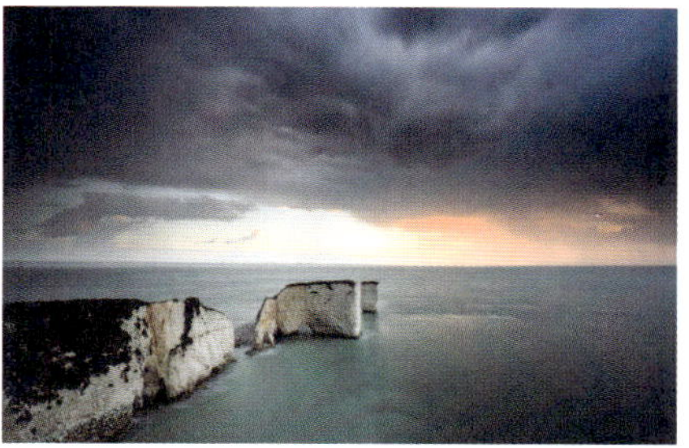

◄ The chalk stacks of Old Harry Rocks in Dorset, England, are a well-known local landmark and a popular spot for landscape photographers. The most popular view is of the cliffs stretching out to sea with Old Harry at the end.

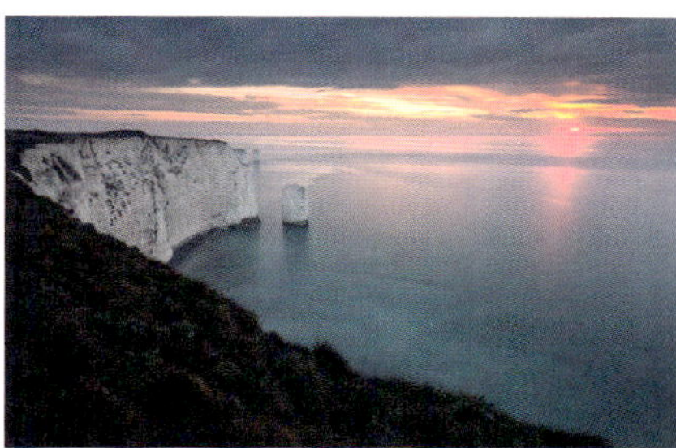

◄ By walking just a couple of hundred yards, I was able to find this alternative viewpoint (left and bottom), which is no less dramatic and—being less familiar—is perhaps more eye-catching.

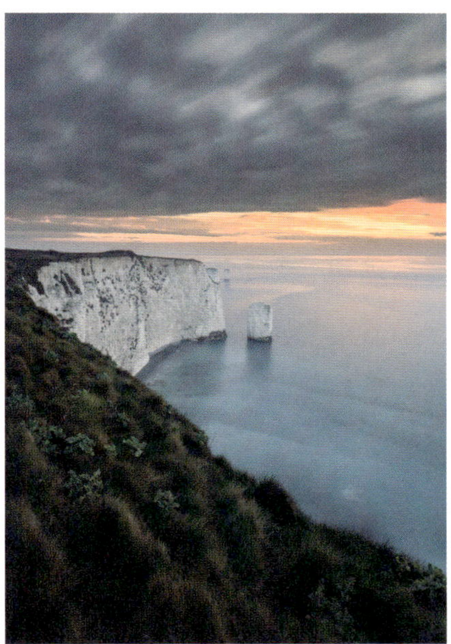

FIELD NOTES

- Familiarize yourself with the well-known viewpoints and then start looking for possible alternatives, using maps, apps, and online resources. Check what times of the day and year might best suit the viewpoint—apps such as The Photographer's Ephemeris and PhotoPills are excellent resources.

- Visit the location without your camera, so you don't get tempted to start shooting as soon as you see something you like—there may be a better shot around the corner. Once you have checked the potential viewpoints and compositions, return with your camera on a suitable day.

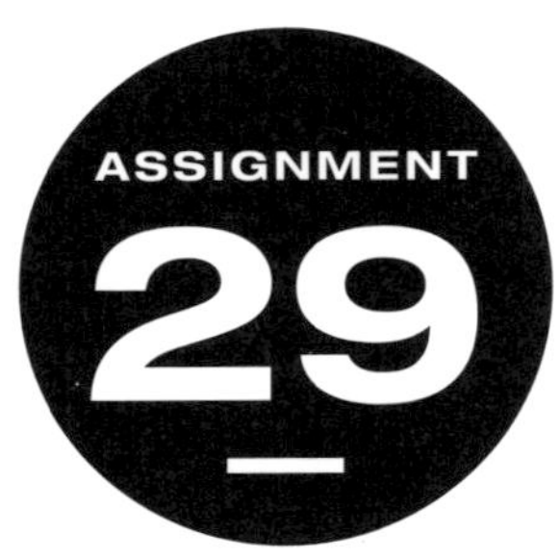

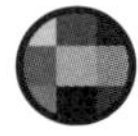

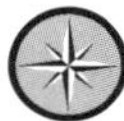
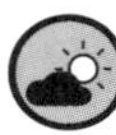

SPECIAL KIT

- A pair of comfortable shoes

TIPS

- You don't need sweeping vistas—look for abstract and detail shots as well.

- Work with the natural character of the landscape—for example, if there aren't many striking features, try minimalist compositions (see page 16).

▶ *This was shot just a 15-minute drive from my home. It's a scene you could easily ignore—during the day it's a pretty but unremarkable view next to a car park. However, shoot on the right morning—with the river still, some color in the sky, and rising mist—and get close to the boats with a telephoto lens, and it looks stunning.*

STAY LOCAL

It's tempting to think that you have to travel a long way to shoot landscapes and that only epic vistas will translate into great shots; that a shot only has value if it has been hard to create and shooting close to home is somehow "cheating." However, there are great landscapes everywhere, and you shouldn't overlook your local patch, even if it isn't home to snow-capped mountains, glaciers, or vast sand dunes.

There are many advantages to staying close to home: you can visit whenever you like, often at a moment's notice (useful in changeable weather), and you can really get to know the best time and weather conditions in which to capture your locations. In this way, you can build up a comprehensive portfolio. Plus there is the benefit of reduced cost—little or no fuel to pay for, no hotel or food bills—and a limited carbon footprint.

So, this assignment is all about showing off your local area with a series of stunning shots. Ideally, these should be taken within walking distance of your home, but if this really isn't feasible, then limit yourself to a 20-minute drive.

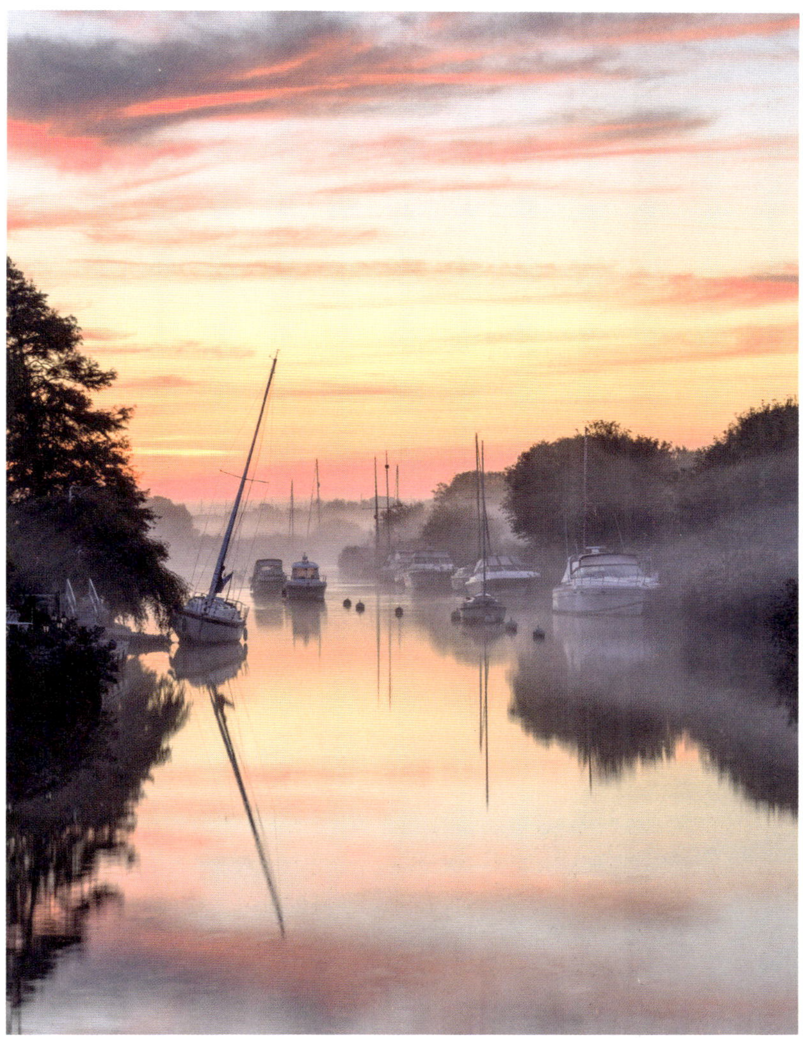

FIELD NOTES

When exploring your neighborhood, work out which conditions will suit different viewpoints. All landscape photographs depend on weather conditions—even the classic locations will look dull in the wrong light. Try to visualize which locations will look good in the golden hours, which might suit the blue hour, which could look good in fog, and so on. And then go back with your camera at those times.

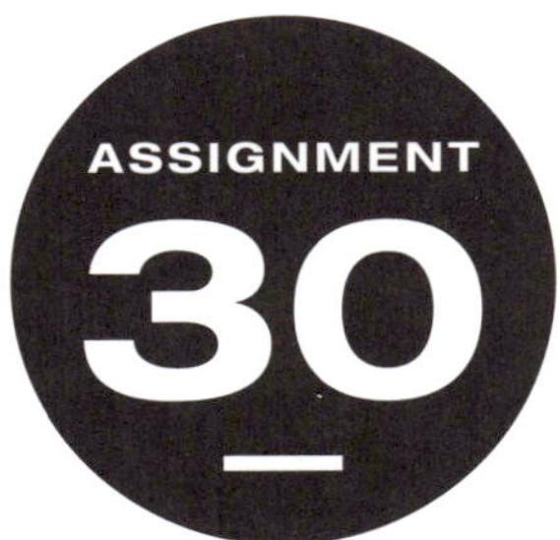

ASSIGNMENT 30

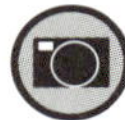

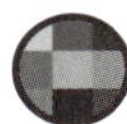

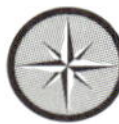

SPECIAL KIT

- Polarizing filter

TIPS

- Always attach a polarizing filter when photographing woodland. Rotate the filter until glare reflecting off the leaves is reduced or eliminated, and natural saturation restored.

- Short telephoto lens lengths (about 60–100mm) are well suited to woodland photography, allowing photographers to isolate areas of the scene and create more refined compositions.

▼ *Spring is one of the best times of year to photograph woodland.*

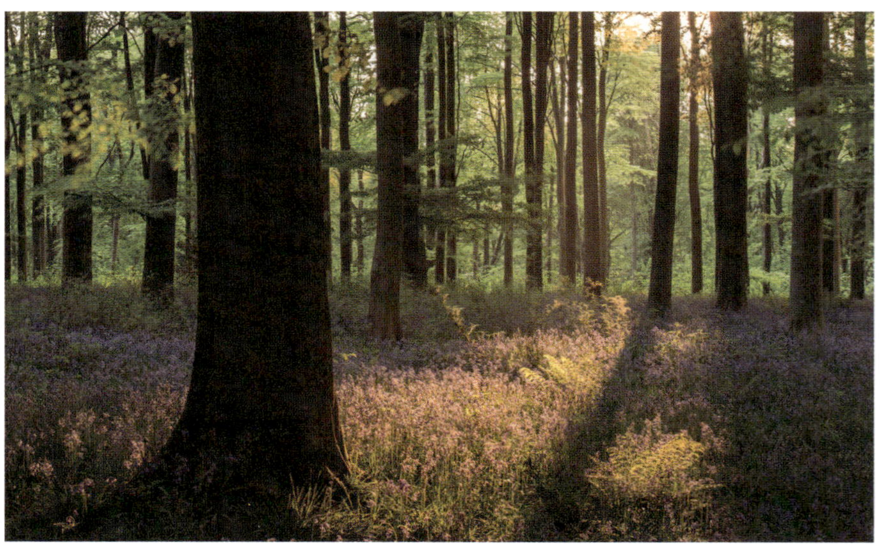

INTO THE WOODS

If you go down to the woods today, you're sure of a big surprise! Woodland interiors are full of picture potential, and for this assignment you will need to visit a local wood in pursuit of photos. The appearance of woodland can vary tremendously depending on its age and size, and also the season. Ancient deciduous woodland will typically provide the best photo opportunities, but rows of regimental conifer plantations can also create striking photographs.

Unsurprisingly, spring and fall tend to be the best times of year to shoot woodland interiors. During spring, foliage is fresh and vibrant, while your shots might also benefit from seasonal carpets of flowers. Meanwhile, in fall, the green pigment (chlorophyll) breaks down, revealing fiery colors (carotenoids and anthocyanins). Dry, sunny weather combined with cool nights trigger this intense, photogenic palette of red, yellow, and orange. The best fall color tends to be during October and November in the Northern Hemisphere.

▼ Have fun with your photography. If you are using a zoom lens, for instance, rotate the zoom ring during exposure to create a zoom burst effect (see page 114).

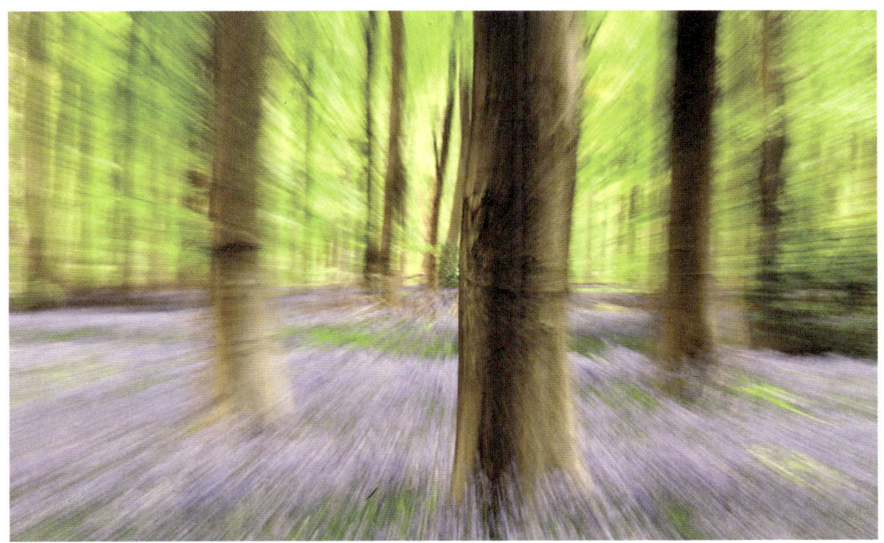

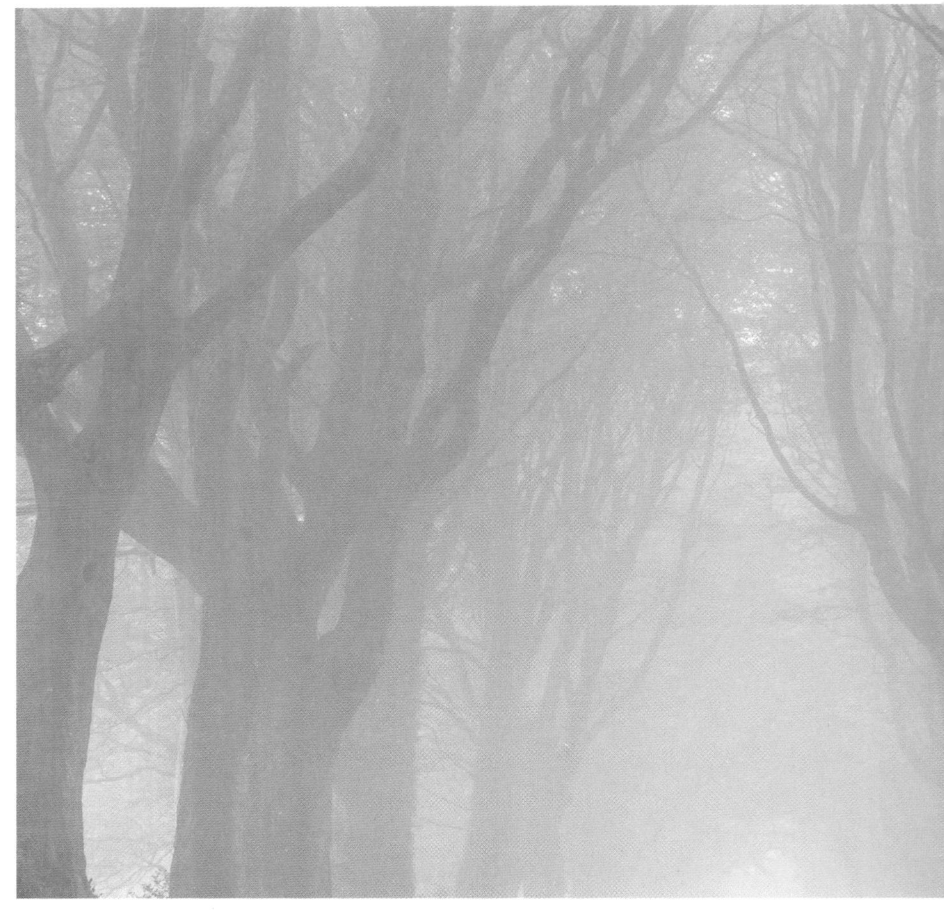

INSPIRATION

- Regardless of what time of year you decide to shoot woodland, light is the key. Although less dramatic, the flat light on cloudy, overcast days suits woodland photography. Contrast is low, helping the camera to capture rich, authentic colors.

- Low morning or evening sunlight can create truly stunning conditions in woodland, backlighting foliage and filtering between trunks. Low sunlight will cast long, inky shadows across the woodland floor, and you can use these compositionally as compelling foreground interest and lead-in lines.

- Visit when it is misty. Not only will fog help simplify the look of woodland, but it will add mood and mystery, and even give your shots an eerie feeling.

FIELD NOTES

- Avoid bright, overhead sunlight when shooting woodland interiors. Sun-dappled woodland floors might look good to the human eye, but a high level of contrast will make it tricky for your camera to record both highlight and shadow detail.

- Woodland is a truly chaotic environment, and one that photographers often struggle with compositionally. Without forethought and care, your shots can look messy and lack focus. Keep compositions simple and look for balance and order. Try using pathways, rivers, a fallen trunk, or a stump to help anchor your composition—this will create a point of interest and imply depth.

- Don't just shoot conventional viewpoints. Lie on your back and shoot upward with a wideangle or fisheye lens to exaggerate the height of trees and make them appear more imposing.

- You can also try some intentional camera movement (ICM) (see page 114), or even a zoom burst. By zooming the lens during the exposure, you can create streaks of color and light bursting from the center of the frame.

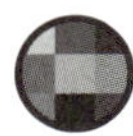

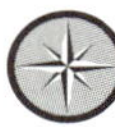

SPECIAL KIT

- Polarizing filter

TIPS

- To enhance the colors of flowers, attach a polarizing filter and shoot after rainfall, when blooms and foliage are at their vivid best.

- To generate a large enough depth of field to keep both your foreground flowers and the background sharp, select a small aperture in the region of f/11 or f/16.

- If a small aperture doesn't provide sufficient depth of field, consider focus-stacking (see page 35).

▼ *Flowers will enliven your landscape photos, particularly when they grow en masse.*

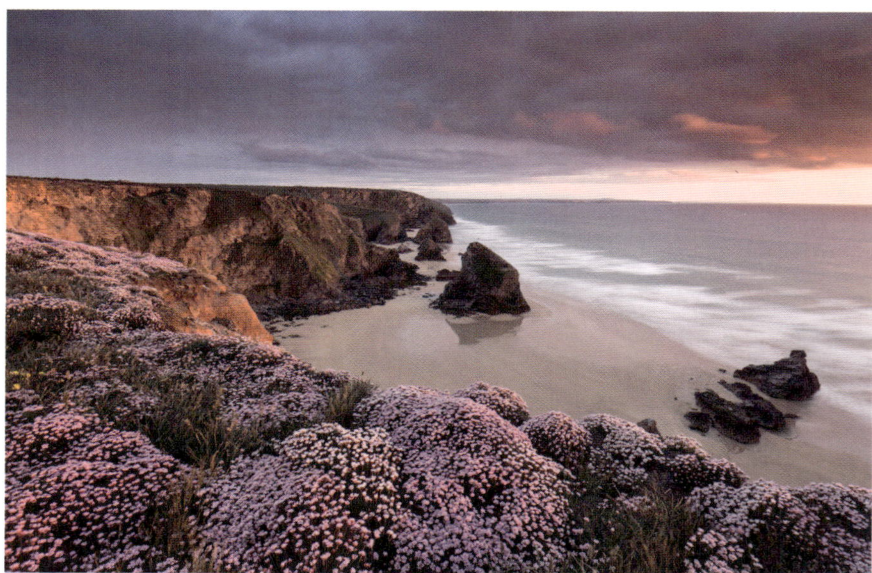

FLOWER POWER

Your brief here is to create a set of stunning flower photographs. Flowers are popular subjects, but are mostly shot in frame-filling close-up. Don't overlook their potential to provide colorful foreground interest in broad vistas. During spring and summer, flowers can be found growing in huge numbers at coastal cliff-tops, in woodlands, or as cultivated crops. They add color impact and create depth, texture, and context.

Flowers are ephemeral things, so timing is important—do your research first and visit when the display is close to its best, and before crops are harvested. The optimum time can vary from year to year, so monitor progress by making repeat visits.

Flowers can enhance your landscapes in various ways. They can act as an entry point to the scene beyond, or provide the main focus for your shot. Camera height, orientation, and perspective are all important. Low viewpoints tend to work well, placing emphasis on colorful foreground blooms. By using an ultra-wideangle or even a fisheye lens you will be able to distort perspective and make foreground blooms appear more prominent. To emphasize the color and density of a carpet of flowers, try shooting from slightly further away with a short or medium telephoto lens instead—this will foreshorten perspective and exaggerate the intensity of the color.

▼ *Have fun with different focal lengths and perspectives. In this instance, I used an 8mm fisheye lens for a quirky result.*

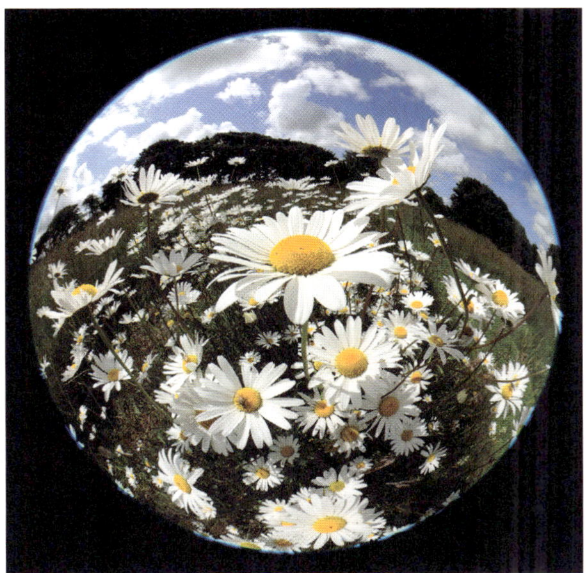

FIELD NOTES

Wind speed is an important consideration. To avoid delicate flowers being blown and blurred in your photographs, take photos when the wind speed is below 15mph (24kph), and if necessary, increase ISO to generate a shutter speed fast enough to record them sharply. Sometimes, though, a little subject motion can be attractive.

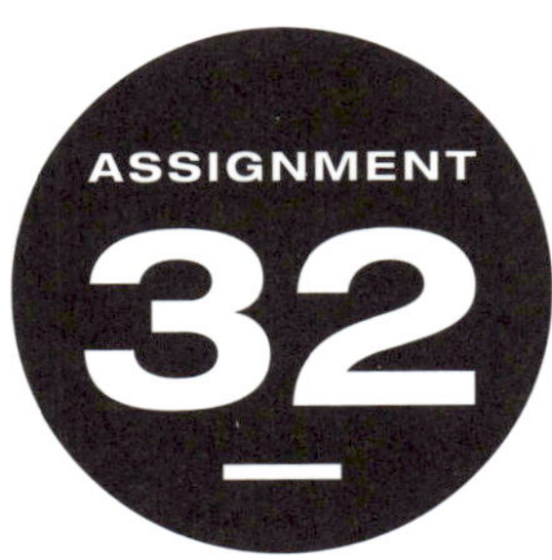

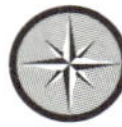

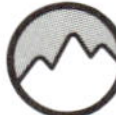

TIPS

- Side-lighting will help to give depth and volume to buildings.

- All landscapes look good when shot in the golden hour, but buildings really come to life when shot in warm, golden light.

- Make use of lead-in lines to draw the viewer's attention from the foreground to the building.

- Shooting from a high viewpoint can help to show the building in its setting.

- It can be worth waiting until dusk to see if any lights come on in the building; the contrast between the warm light within and the cool ambient light can be very photogenic.

▼ *Buildings generally look best with side-lighting, which adds depth and volume. The ruined church in an otherwise empty landscape creates a real sense of isolation.*

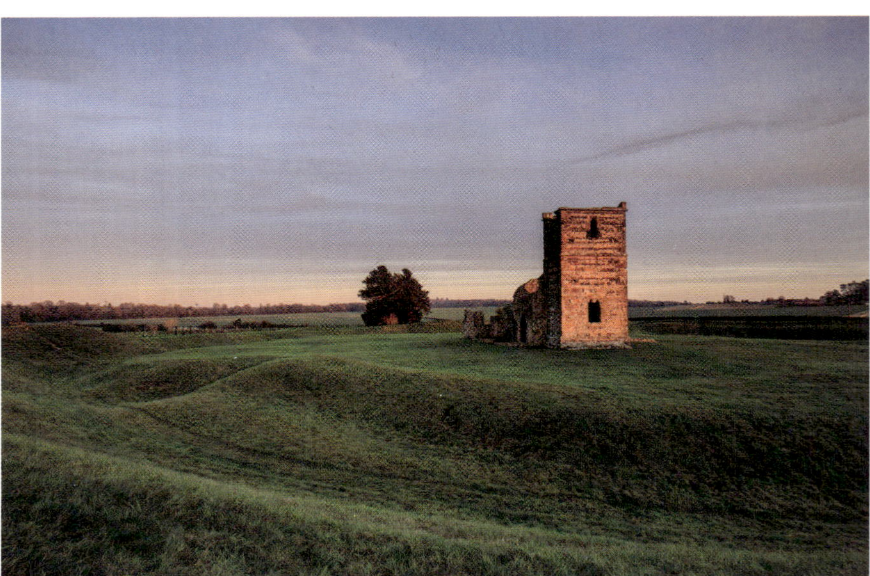

SHOOT BUILDINGS

There is a beauty in the untouched landscape and many photographers try to avoid including buildings in an attempt to suggest wilderness and isolation. However, human influence on the landscape is extensive and buildings can add a lot to a scene. So, for this assignment you should actively look to include buildings in your landscape photographs.

Buildings can offer a sense of scale for background mountains. They can provide a focal point, which catches the viewer's attention and gives the eye somewhere to rest, creating a sense of completion. They can give a sense of place. The human element can also add a hint of storytelling to your image—for example, a lone building in apparent wilderness suggests isolation. Different types of building tell different stories: a ruined building, overgrown with foliage, shows nature reclaiming the landscape, whereas a modern building in the countryside indicates humans trying to impose themselves on nature.

When working on this assignment, look for buildings that suggest different narratives, and for buildings that sit comfortably in their surroundings, as well as those that jar in some way with their environment.

▼ *Indigenous architecture can give a sense of place—there are few places in the UK that this could be other than East Anglia.*

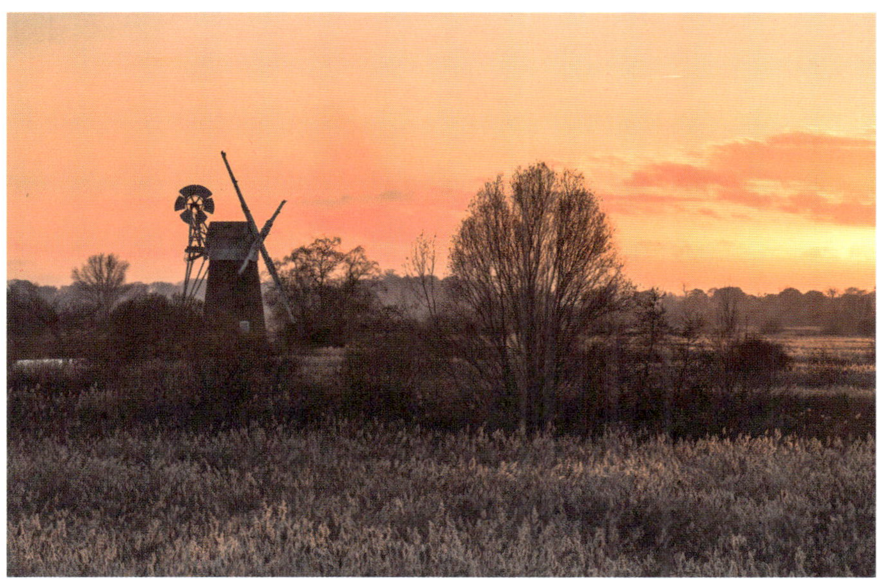

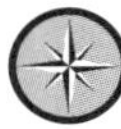

FIELD NOTES

Finding the right viewpoint can help you to find a structured composition, and higher viewpoints are often successful. Bridges are another option, especially as shooting along rivers can bring a sense of order to a composition. Distant views toward city skylines also work well.

SPECIAL KIT

- Tripod

- A range of lenses

- Polarizing filter

TIPS

- Look for interesting details and base your compositions on shapes, colors, and textures.

- Wait until dusk: cities often look their best in the blue hour (see page 32).

- Be creative with modern buildings—shoot from interesting angles, use wideangle lenses, and exploit the effects of distortion. Buildings can look good in harsh light on bright sunny days, so use a polarizing filter.

- Old buildings look best in more traditional landscape light—the golden light first thing in the morning and last thing in the evening.

- Don't ignore the indoors. Shopping malls and covered markets are often interesting, but you may need permission to shoot inside them.

CAPTURE A CITYSCAPE

For many people, landscape photography is all about getting away from the hustle and bustle of town or city life and spending time somewhere peaceful. However, it may be that by doing so they are ignoring some fantastic opportunities in the form of urban landscapes.

The urban environment can be a little overwhelming. Cities are busy, cluttered, constantly changing, with people and vehicles coming and going. Making sense of them can be a challenge, but good composition is all about creating structure out of chaos and the same principles apply to cityscapes: look for strong focal points and ways of directing attention to them, and divide the frame up to create harmony.

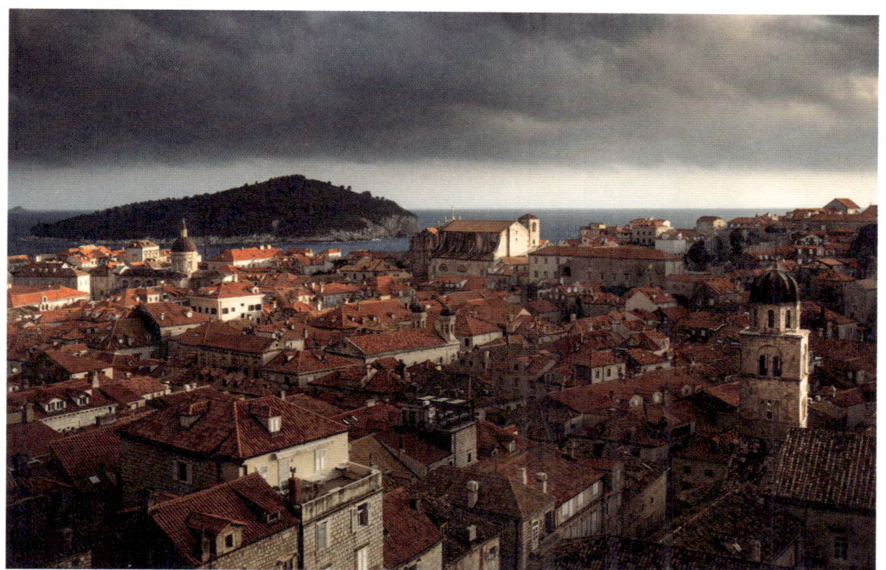

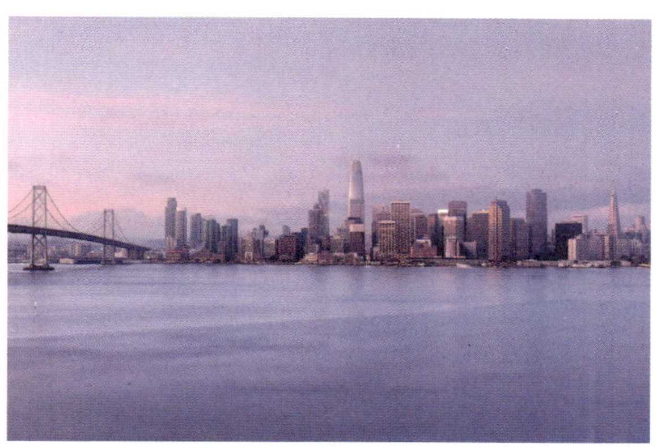

There is an incredible variety of subject matter in the average city: modern architecture, classical architecture, green spaces, and interiors—there will always be something to inspire you. Urban photography is accessible, a little bit different, and can be a real shot in the arm for your creativity.

This is a very straightforward assignment. Your brief is to spend a single day in your nearest city or big town, and to shoot a variety of modern buildings and old buildings. Think about the architecture. Be sure to include exterior and interior shots. You could also use this as an opportunity to practice using contrasts as the basis of your urban landscape compositions (see page 42).

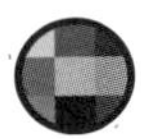

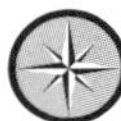
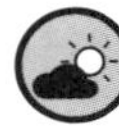

SPECIAL KIT

- Smartphone app for predicting tide times
- Extreme neutral density (ND) filters
- Chamois leather or microfiber cloth

TIPS

- An extreme neutral density (ND) filter, of about 10 stops, can be useful when shooting seaside structures such as piers or a row of groynes.

- In stormy weather, be careful of sea spray—keep a cloth to hand ready to wipe away moisture from lenses and filters.

BESIDE THE SEASIDE

Seaside resorts are full of picture potential. Artificial structures—such as harbor walls, piers, marker posts, seafront arcades, and jetties—add interest to the natural beauty of the sea and sand.

In the summer, resorts tend to be crowded with tourists, making them a tricky place to shoot. However, during wintertime, or in bad weather, coastal resorts tend to be quiet, almost deserted and forlorn. Rough seas and brooding skies can create further interest and atmosphere. Some resorts are particularly colorful, with painted beach huts and illuminated piers just waiting to give your shots immediate impact.

Set yourself the challenge of shooting a series of six great images in a set time— 30 minutes, for example. Any camera type will do—DSLR, mirrorless, compact, or your smartphone's camera—the key ingredient will be color and your use of perspective and creativity. Shoot from low angles, go wide, or maybe use a longer lens to isolate just a small area of interest, such as a door handle or keyhole.

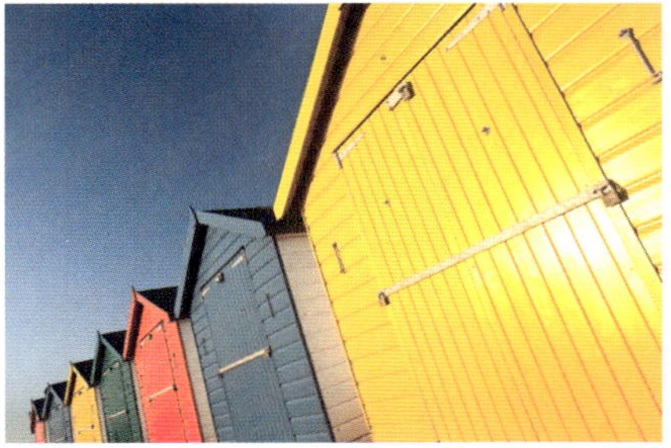 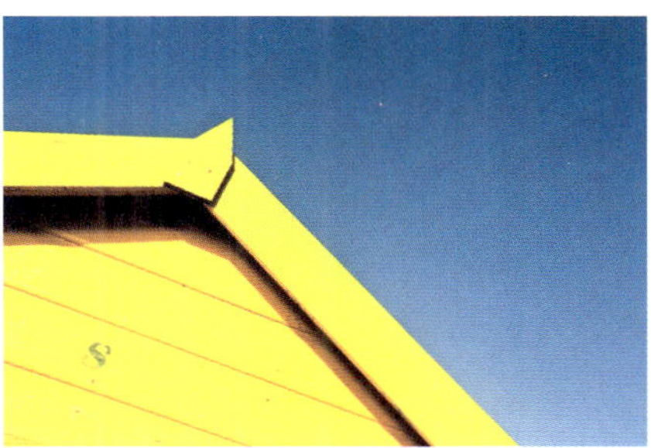

▲ Colorful beach huts make great subjects. Why not set yourself the task of capturing a series of shots within just a short time frame? You don't even need all your gear—your smartphone will suffice.

▼ Bad weather and creatively long exposures will add mood to your seaside landscapes (see page 48).

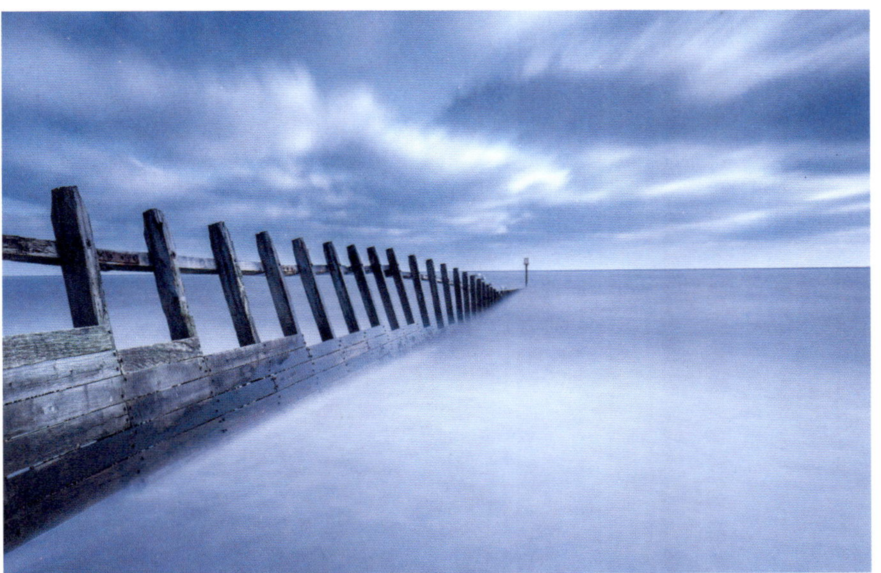

FIELD NOTES

Always be aware of tide times when shooting the coast. Download a dedicated tide app on your smartphone so you always have tidal information to hand. For busy coastal resorts it is often best to visit soon after high water, when the tide is receding and the beach is washed clean of ugly footprints.

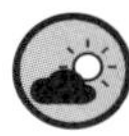

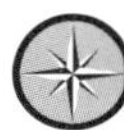

SPECIAL KIT

- Neutral density (ND) and graduated filters
- Rain cover and chamois leather
- Bungee cord

TIPS

- A polarizing filter is useful in rain or drizzle to reduce surface glare.
- On overcast days, graduated filters can inject drama into a sky.
- The low contrast of shots taken in rain or fog means that a high-key treatment in post-processing often makes compelling images.
- On windy days, you will need to shoot with faster shutter speeds, possibly handheld, so increase the ISO and open up your aperture if necessary.

HEAVY WEATHER

The saying "There's no such thing as bad weather, only unsuitable clothing" could be your motto for this assignment. The idea is simply to head out and take some creative shots in bad weather.

Of course, "bad weather" will mean different things to different people, but for most landscape photographers it is probably any conditions where the light doesn't create some relief on the landscape. This could cover anything from dull, flat light on an overcast day through to pouring rain and howling gales.

Match your approach to the conditions. On dull, overcast days, take a trip to the coast and use an extreme neutral density (ND) filter for long exposures. Depending on the length of the exposure and the movement, water can be recorded as an ethereal mist or a glass-like surface. If there are textured clouds above, include lots of sky and try a minimalist composition.

When shooting in rain, set up under cover if possible (or use an umbrella if it's not too windy) and avoid shooting into the wind to keep your lens free of rain drops. Contrast will be low and visibility limited, so look for bold shapes to use as a basis for your composition. A similar approach works in thick fog.

Above all, remember that protecting yourself and your equipment is important. Wear appropriate clothing and try to keep your cameras and lenses dry. If the conditions are really extreme, stay at home.

◄ *It was raining heavily when I shot this image—I was sheltering in a barn. The clouds swirling around the mountains added real atmosphere to the scene.*

FIELD NOTES

- Water and electronics don't mix well, so keep your camera covered. There are plenty of commercial rain covers available, or you can improvise—the shower caps supplied in hotel bathrooms work well. A chamois can be used as a rain cover, and is also useful for wiping kit down if it does get wet.

- In windy conditions, hang your camera bag from your tripod to add extra weight and stability. Attach it via a bungee cord, so the bag sits on the ground and doesn't swing around bumping into the legs and causing even more vibrations.

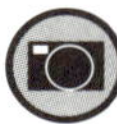

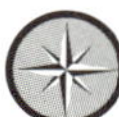
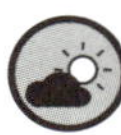

SPECIAL KIT

- Telephoto zoom lens of about 70–300mm

TIPS

- Telephoto lenses are typically best suited to misty conditions. Try using a 70–300mm telephoto zoom lens to condense perspective and exaggerate the mist.

- Just like snow exposures (see page 94), bright mist has a habit of fooling through-the-lens (TTL) metering systems into underexposing a shot. Review your histogram regularly and expect to apply positive exposure compensation to achieve the correct exposure.

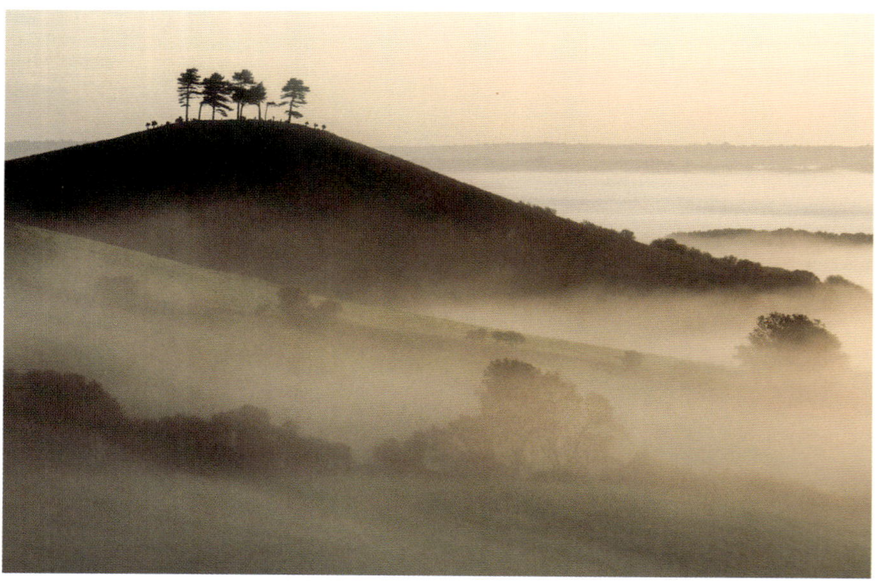

MYSTERIOUS MIST

Mist will simplify the landscape, reducing it to a series of shapes, layers, and outlines. Your assignment is to capture its effect, and then to select your best single shot. Look for an obvious focal point to either isolate or use as an anchor for your composition—maybe a landmark, boat, animal, or shapely tree. Shooting from a lower level, down amongst the mist, can also produce stunning results. As you will soon discover, results can appear high-key and almost monochromatic.

Mist and fog can occur at any time of the year, but they are most likely during spring and fall. The most appealing type for photography is "radiation fog," which forms during clear, still nights due to the ground losing heat via radiation. In simple terms, the ground cools nearby air to saturation point and an attractive white layer of mist forms. Although it is impossible to predict just where and when mist will occur, or how dense it will be, by studying the weather forecast you will increase your chances of success. Look for cool, clear nights with a low wind speed, then set your alarm clock for an early start the following morning.

You will need to think carefully about location choice. Elevated viewpoints above the fog provide vistas of the mist hanging evocatively in valleys and immersing countryside and villages. You may even witness a cloud inversion when the combination of cold temperatures and high pressure create dense low-level mist, with only hills and peaks poking up above it. Large bodies of water can act like mist generators in the right conditions, so opting for a viewpoint overlooking a lake will enhance your chances.

◀ *A combination of a high vantage point
and a telephoto lens will suit this assignment.*

FIELD NOTES

- When you set your alarm, allow extra driving time as your journey is likely to be slower due to poor driving conditions and reduced visibility.

- Mist can rise or evaporate quickly, so work efficiently to make the most of the rapidly changing conditions.

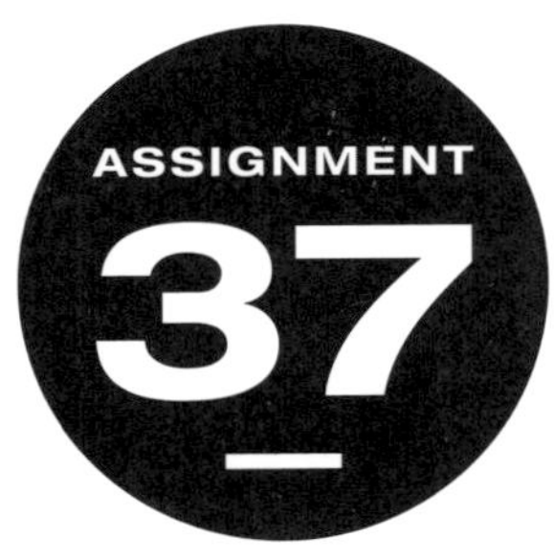

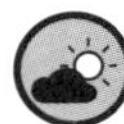

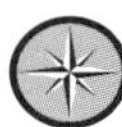

SPECIAL KIT

- Polarizing filter

- Lens hood

- Rain cover

- Chamois leather or microfiber cloth

- Waterproof clothing

TIPS

- Use a polarizing filter to enhance the rainbow—simply rotate the filter until you see the rainbow "pop."

- Keep a constant eye on your lens or filter to make sure there are no rain drops that might ruin your pictures—wipe them clean with a good-quality microfiber cloth.

- A lens hood can help keep your lens clear.

▶ *Strong composition is just as important when photographing rainbows as at any other time. Here, although it meant only including a part of the rainbow, the shot was stronger with clear foreground interest and the distant headland placed near an intersection of thirds.*

FIELD NOTES

- The best way to capture a rainbow is to set up in a shower and wait for it to clear—if you set up after the rain finishes, you will be in a rush, and risk missing the best moments.

- You will need to protect your kit, so use a rain cover and have a microfiber cloth or chamois leather handy to wipe your equipment down. Avoid changing lenses in the rain—make sure you do this in a sheltered spot before you set up.

- A rainbow may appear during rain, so protect your camera and lenses. If it is impossible to keep your lens completely clean, take multiple shots: the drops will be in different places on each image, so you can merge them to create a single clean shot.

CHASING RAINBOWS

Who doesn't love a rainbow? They are a beautiful sight and their relative rarity gives them added appeal. They are formed when sunlight passes through rain, with the raindrops acting as tiny prisms—when light reflects off the drops, it is broken down into a spectrum. Rainbows appear directly opposite the sun and can be full circles, although we usually only see an arc.

Your mission is to shoot a rainbow! You will need to head out on days when the forecast is for sunshine and showers. The shots with most impact are usually taken in clearing showers, as the rainbow will be set against a dark, brooding sky, and the clarity of the scene—with the air having been washed clean by the rain—can be outstanding. Of course, this provides a few challenges, such as getting wet, so make sure you wear suitable clothing.

Rainbows can be fleeting, so it is often necessary to work fast. With such a naturally beautiful phenomenon it can also be easy to forget that the usual rules of composition still apply. So, take particular care with this aspect of the image, making sure all the elements are balanced and harmonious. Luckily, it's relatively easy to predict when a rainbow might appear, and you can work out exactly where it will form, so try to set up in advance and frame a suitable composition while you wait for it.

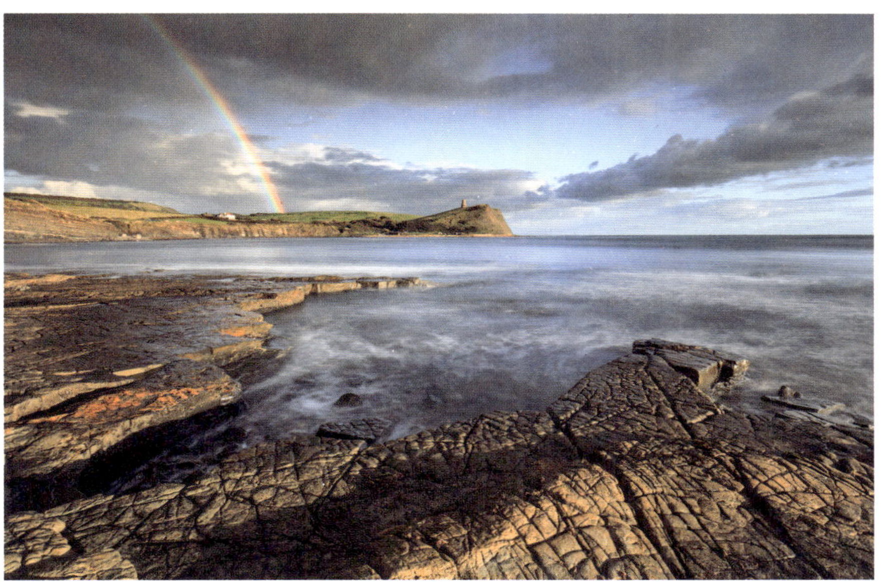

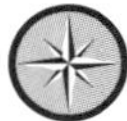

SPECIAL KIT

- Telephoto lens
- Neutral density (ND), ultraviolet (UV) filters
- Rain cover
- Chamois leather or microfiber cloth
- Lens cloth and cleaning fluid
- Tripod
- Smartphone app for predicting tide times

TIPS

- Exposures that are too long can reduce the impact of shots—water that looks "misty" suggests tranquility rather than power.
- Protect your camera and lens with a rain cover, and wipe your lens and filter regularly. Carry lens cloths and cleaning fluid, and use a UV filter to protect the lens.

STORMY SEAS

Observing the raw power of nature can be a humbling experience and few things demonstrate that power as spectacularly as waves crashing onto the coast during a big storm. Capturing these moments can result in compelling images that contain beautiful patterns and textures.

To really show the size and power of the waves, shoot them as they crash against an artificial object—for example, a harbor wall, lighthouse, or pier. Not only will this give an indication of scale, but it is also a powerful symbol of the constant battle against natural forces. Big waves move quickly, so faster shutter speeds are normally recommended to freeze the breaking waves as they form interesting shapes and throw spray across the scene. Set your camera drive to its fastest continuous setting, and trigger the shutter just before a wave breaks—keep shooting until the wave recedes. Slower shutter speeds of up to 1 sec. can also be effective, softening the waves and creating swirling patterns, while still keeping their basic shape.

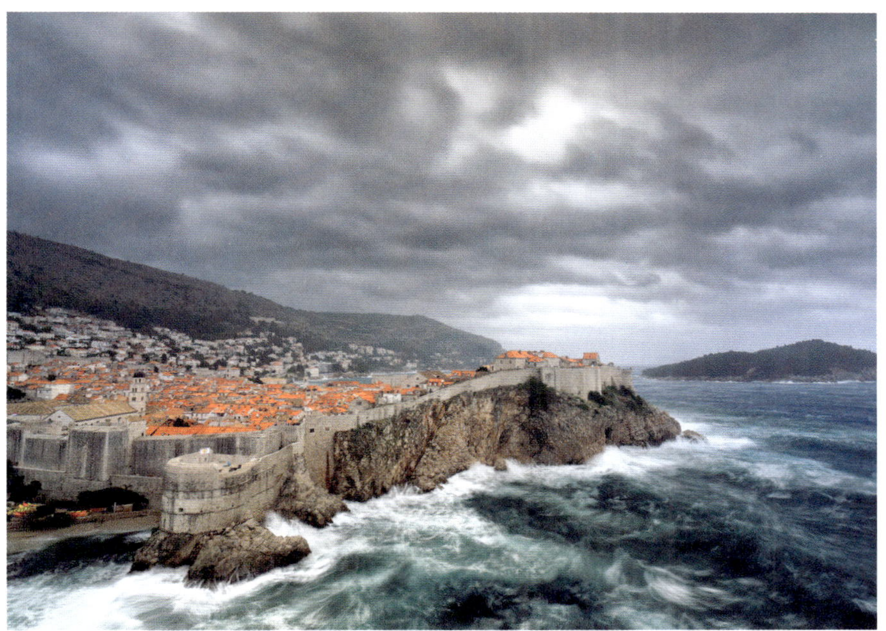

▲ *A shutter speed of around 1 sec. has created swirling patterns in the angry sea as waves crash against the city walls of Dubrovnik Old Town. Including the surroundings helps to show the scale of the waves.*

For a more abstract result, shoot the waves without the context of coastal architecture, concentrating on shapes, textures, and patterns created by the sea.

For this assignment, head to the coast when a storm is forecast, with the aim of creating a set of images using a variety of shutter speeds. Capture the waves with their surroundings, as well as in more abstract compositions.

FIELD NOTES

- Safety comes first. Every year, a number of people tragically lose their lives because they have underestimated the power of the sea. Position yourself at a safe distance—ideally from a high viewpoint—and shoot with a telephoto lens. Before you set up, spend some time observing the sea, making sure that you really are out of reach of any "rogue" waves and that you have worked out exit routes in case you need them. Check the tide times before you leave and make allowances for incoming tides.

- If possible, shoot at a familiar location. This will help you when it comes to choosing a viewpoint which is both safe and also allows good compositions.

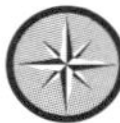
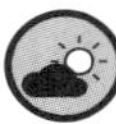

SPECIAL KIT

- Warm clothing

- Rain cover

- Chamois leather or microfiber cloth

- Lens cloth and cleaning fluid

TIPS

- Auto White Balance can render snow with a blue color cast. This can be attractive and enhance the feeling of coldness, but if it's undesirable switch to your camera's Daylight or Cloudy preset (see page 54), or adjust in post-processing.

FIELD NOTES

- When shooting in cold, adverse conditions, it is essential you dress appropriately. Wear good thermal base-layers and warm, waterproof, and windproof outer garments. Hat and gloves are important—your gloves should be thick enough to keep your fingers warm, but thin enough to allow you to operate your camera and adjust filters. Touchscreen or eTip gloves are a good option. Good walking boots are also a must-have.

- Always carry extra batteries, as cold temperatures reduce battery life. Condensation can be an issue too, so keep a lens cloth close to hand and gently wipe away any moisture before triggering the shutter.

- If you need to change the lens, make the switch as quickly as possible, and change the lens with the body facing downward to avoid snow entering the camera.

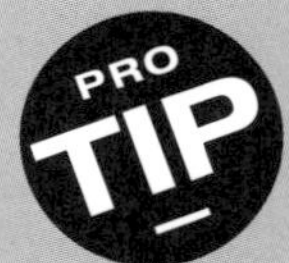

EXPOSURE

Being reflective and white, snow can confuse camera metering systems into underexposing. This will make your snowy images appear dark and dull. To compensate, increase the exposure by +1 exposure value (EV).

Use your camera's histogram to help you judge exposure. Histograms provide a tonal representation of a scene, so when shooting bright snow, graphs will naturally be bunched to the right. However, the histogram must not be overflowing off the far right of the graph—this would mean overexposure and clipped highlights.

LET IT SNOW

For this winter assignment, your brief is to experiment with the challenges and creative possibilities presented by snow. Snowfall can simplify the landscape, reducing it to a series of photogenic shapes, while disguising artificial objects or hiding ugly features. Virgin snow and hoar frost clinging to every branch and twig can create magical conditions. Depending on where you live, cold spells can either be guaranteed or brief. Either way, you need to be prepared to make the most of the conditions. Always dress appropriately for the weather—if you get cold, the desire to get warm and comfortable will overtake the urge to be creative.

The best snowy landscapes are typically when the powder is fresh and untouched. If snow is forecast overnight, get up early and capture images that are free from human footprints. Think carefully about where you tread, being careful not to step anywhere you might later want to photograph. Tracks, pathways, and roads can act as useful lead-in lines in wintry landscapes.

Capture a range of images. Snow lends itself to black-and-white conversion, or you could include a walker wearing brightly colored clothing to introduce a splash of color and add interest and context. Snow also reflects natural light and color in the sky—so, for truly magical snowy images, shoot during the golden hours of sunlight.

▼ *A strong focal point will strengthen the impact of your snowy landscape images.*

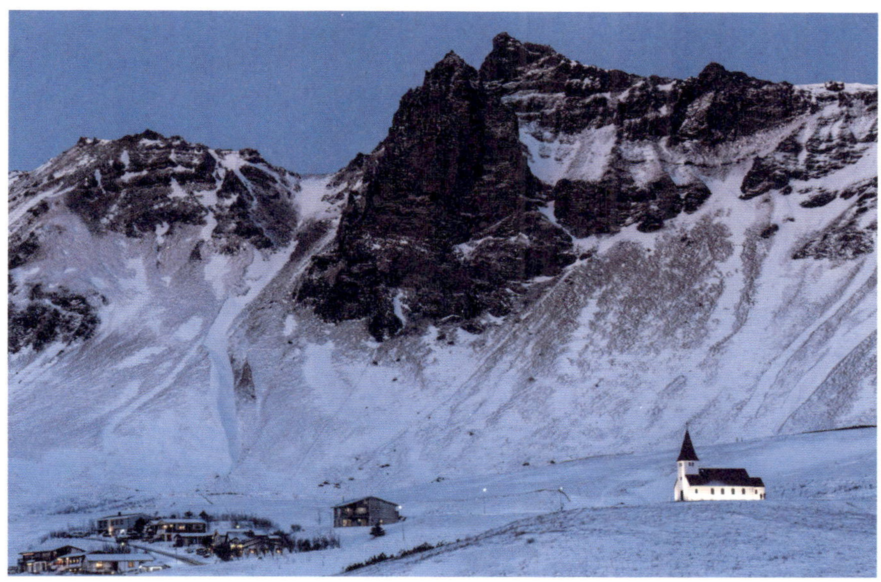

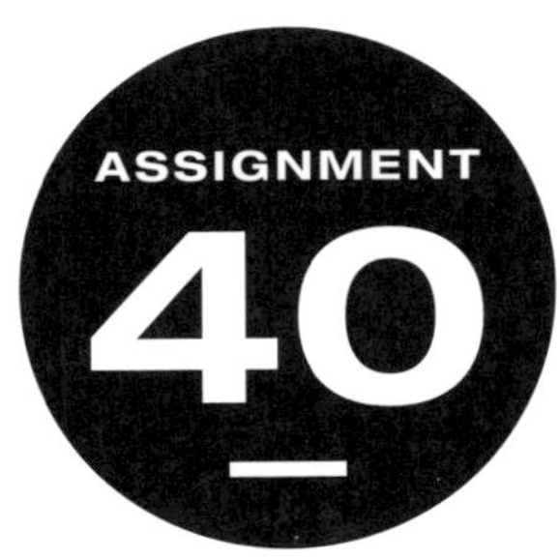

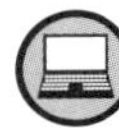

SPECIAL KIT

- Polarizing filter

- Post-processing software, such as Adobe Lightroom or Nik Silver Efex Pro

TIPS

- Base your compositions on contrast, shape, and texture.

- Long exposures including moving water are often successful, as this creates a natural tonal contrast between white water and darker areas.

- Use a polarizing filter to enhance contrast and deep blue skies, which convert well to black and white.

- Don't worry about noise. A lot of black-and-white films are quite grainy and a little noise in a mono image can add to the atmosphere.

MONO MAGIC

It may not be immediately obvious, but this is an assignment that will help you focus on the fundamentals of composition: shape, line, texture, and contrast. Without the distraction of color, these are the features that become important. They do, in fact, also underpin most color compositions, but in black-and-white they are vital ingredients of a successful shot.

Very few people are able to pre-visualize images in black and white, so things to look for include a full range of tones and textures—for example, skies with layered clouds often convert well—as well as bold, graphic shapes. Simple, uncluttered compositions work best, so try to find strong lines and angles, and clear, obvious focal points.

Working in tones rather than color can cause problems because of the way certain colors translate to grayscale—red and green, for example, can look very similar in monochrome. This impacts upon composition, as separating elements in the image can become tricky without color. Carefully compose a series of images, so there is enough physical separation—again, keeping things as simple as possible.

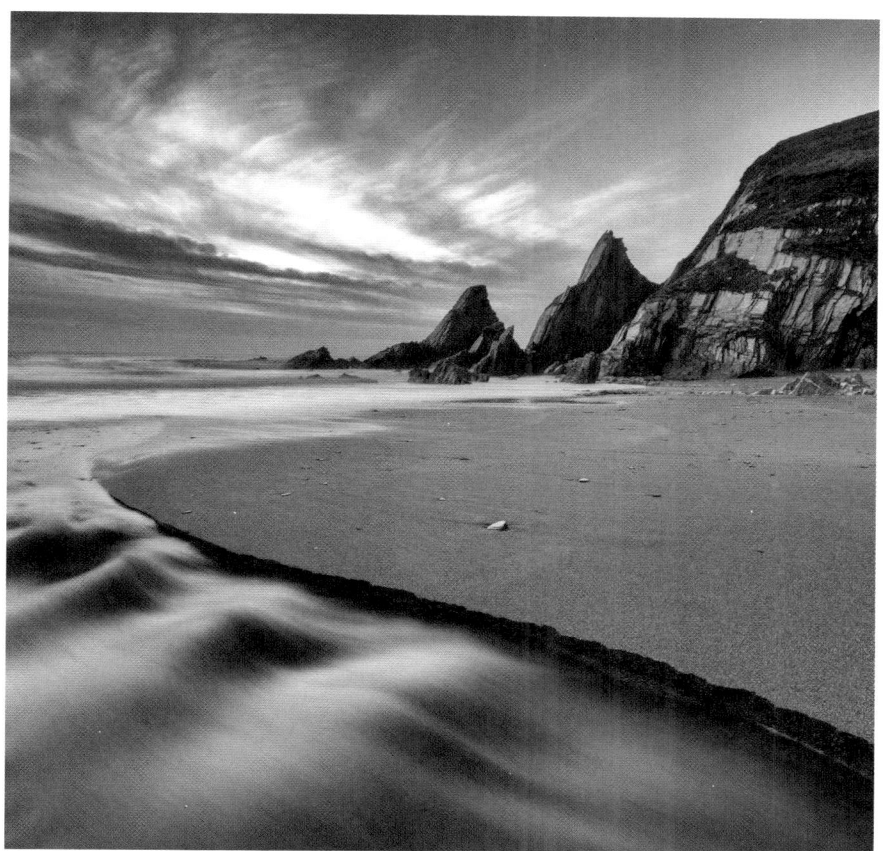

▲ *Bold, graphic compositions and a full range of tones and textures will help to make successful black-and-white images.*

There are many ways to convert color images to monochrome, but using the Black and White mix in Adobe Lightroom (part of the Hue, Saturation, Luminance controls) provides a lot of control and allows you to mimic the effects of the color filters used in black-and-white film photography. Alternatively, there are some excellent specialist apps, such as DxO's Silver Efex Pro plugin from its Nik Collection.

FIELD NOTES

If you really struggle to "see" in black and white, try using your camera's monochrome picture style. Then, using Live View on a DSLR or the electronic viewfinder (EVF) of a mirrorless camera, you can view the scene in black and white and assess its potential. This won't affect the Raw image, which will still be recorded in color.

41

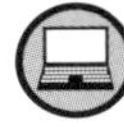

SPECIAL KIT

- Infrared filter, such as a Hoya R72

- Tripod

TIPS

- Metering is not always accurate when using an infrared (IR) filter, so check the playback histogram and be prepared to reshoot.

- To compensate for the loss of light you can increase the ISO. Don't worry too much about noise, as infrared film was very grainy, so this just adds to the "character" of infrared photographs.

- If your end result is to be monochrome, set your in-camera picture style to mono—this won't affect the Raw file, but will help you preview how well the image will convert.

▶ *For the best results, consider getting a camera converted. In this example, shot with a converted Canon EOS 1D MkII, the sky has turned black and the foliage is a very pale white.*

INFRARED FUN

Shooting infrared (IR) is a great project for the summer months, when many landscape photographers struggle to find subjects, because of the high sun and harsh, high-contrast light. However, these conditions are perfect for infrared photography, especially black-and-white infrared; blue skies are rendered as a deep black, which contrasts strikingly with clouds, while foliage turns a ghostly white. Infrared images are very eye-catching, often with an otherworldly look to them, and this assignment invites you to explore the possibilities they offer.

Digital cameras do not see infrared light as they have IR-blocking filters in front of the sensor to help them achieve natural-looking color. You can have a camera converted (which is both permanent and quite expensive), or you can fit an infrared filter, such as a Hoya R72 in front of the lens. This blocks all light from the visible

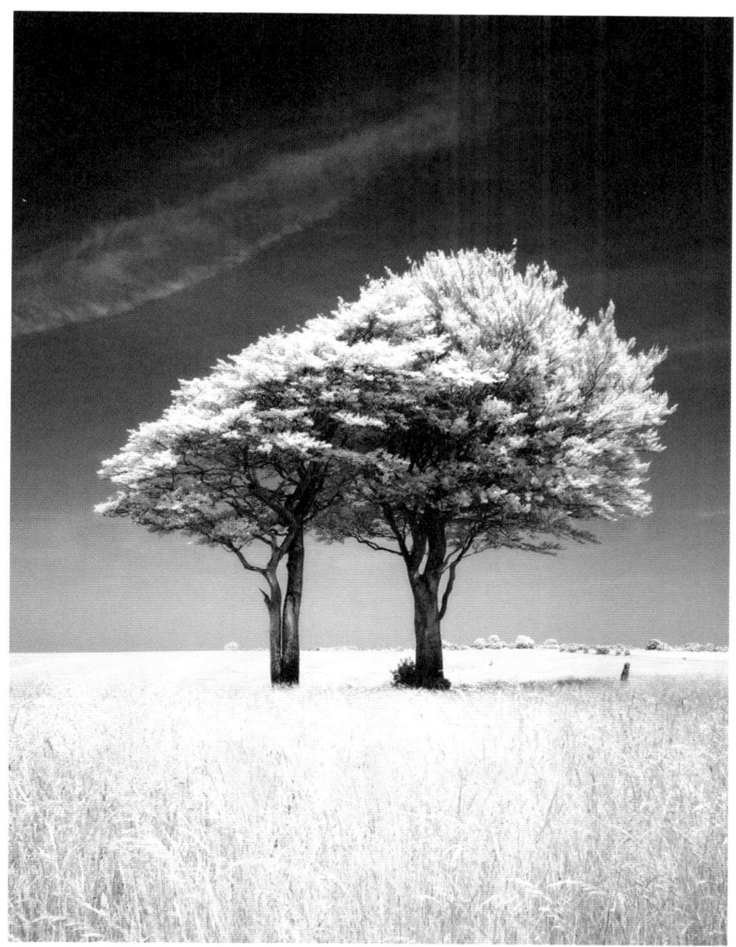

spectrum, leaving only infrared light to reach the sensor. This is the cheaper option, but the trade-off is that, because of the camera's IR-blocking filter, long exposures are required to create an image. Exactly how long depends on your camera as different brands have different strengths of IR-blocking filter, but you can expect to it to be similar to shooting with a 10-stop neutral density filter.

Infrared images require careful post-processing. If you are shooting in Raw, you will have a color infrared image. So, to achieve the "false color" look, you will need to switch the Red and Blue channels in Photoshop—there are plenty of online tutorials to show you how to do this. If you are converting to mono, increase the contrast and also add a diffuse glow to the highlights, which will recreate the look of classic infrared film. Complete your assignment with prints of your six best shots.

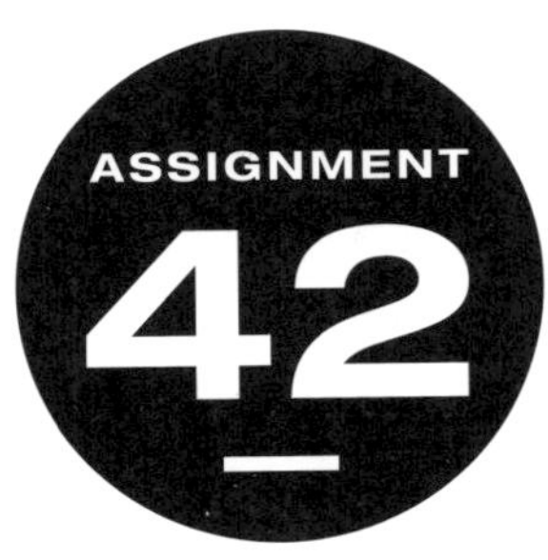

SPECIAL KIT

- Film camera

- Rolls of color and/or black-and-white film

TIPS

- If you buy film in any quantity, prolong its lifespan by keeping it refrigerated.

- Digital sensors are better at recovering shadow detail than highlights. Negative film is the opposite—retaining highlight detail but recording less shadow information. Therefore, err on the side of overexposure.

- You shouldn't have any issues finding a good professional lab where you can get film developed. Search online or enquire at a local photography store. Most labs will develop your film and scan the negatives so you have a digital copy.

SHOOT FILM

Film has been around for almost 200 years, but have you ever shot a roll? Depending on your age and experience, there is a good chance you have only ever known digital capture. But for this assignment, we encourage you to return to the classic medium of 35mm film. There is something magical about exposing film, and getting back to basics is not only a good discipline, but a fun and rewarding experience. Because you have to treat film with more respect than digital, you tend to slow down, think more, and shoot less. This will help you to refine and perfect your technique.

If you don't already have a film camera gathering dust in a cupboard somewhere, visit a thrift store or look on an auction site like eBay. Top-quality 35mm SLRs can be purchased for very little, and within days you can be exposing silver halide. Like vinyl in the music world, film is having a renaissance and there is a wide variety of color and black-and-white negative films readily available online. If you like mono, Ilford HP5 and Kodak T-Max 100 are popular choices, or perhaps try Kodak Portra if you favor color. Load your film into the camera and you are ready to have some fun...

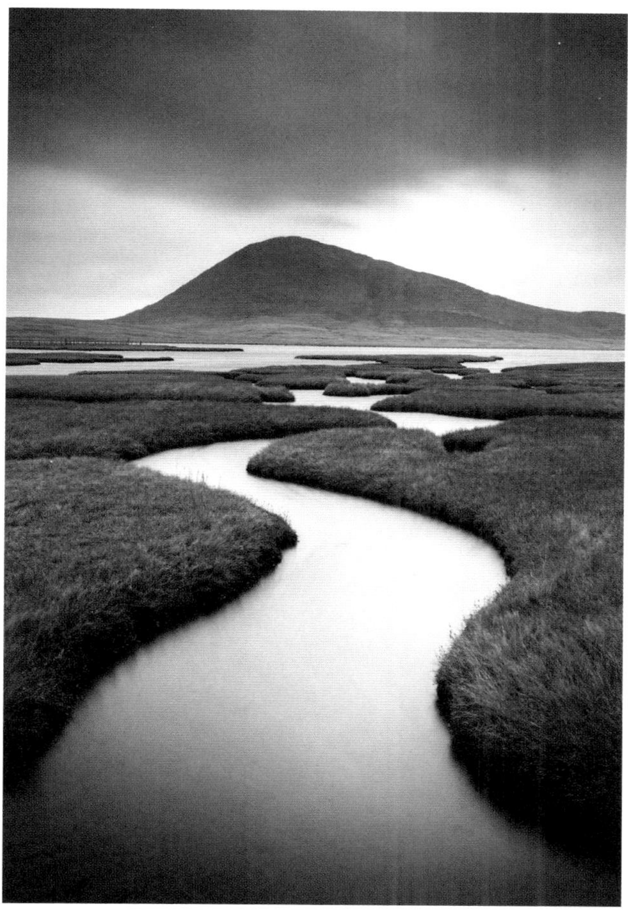

▲ *We already spend too much time in front of a screen, but with film you just shoot, send the film away, and wait. There's no fuss or editing required, just back-to-basics photography. Try it for yourself.*

FIELD NOTES

Loading a roll of 35mm film is quite straightforward. Open the film back, place the roll on the left, and pull the leader across to a white or red dot (for auto-loading cameras) or thread it on the spool at the right before closing the back. Motorized cameras will wind to the first frame automatically, but you will need to use the thumb lever to wind and shoot one or two blank frames on older cameras.

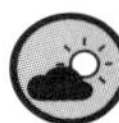

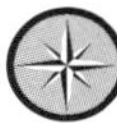

SPECIAL KIT

- A wideangle lens with a fast maximum aperture

- Sturdy tripod

- Smartphone app for predicting star positions, such as PhotoPills

TIPS

- To get enough light on the sensor you will need to shoot at a high ISO (as high as 3200) and at your lens' widest aperture.

- Your lens should be focused at infinity. The easiest way to do this is to find infinity focus in daylight and tape the focusing ring to keep it in position.

- If shooting the Milky Way, you need as little ambient light as possible, so a new moon is best. For the Northern Lights, some moonlight will help to add interest by lighting up the foreground.

SHOOTING STARS

Nighttime photography has become extremely popular because of the excellent low-light performance of modern digital cameras. Your assignment is to head out after dark and shoot the Milky Way, the Northern Lights, and meteor showers!

The night sky is an alluring subject, but it is not an easy one to capture. Unless you are shooting star trails, you need to keep stars sharp so that they appear as points of light. To calculate the maximum exposure length for rendering them sharp, use the "500 rule"—divide 500 by the focal length you're shooting at. For instance, 500 divided by 20 is 25, so 25 seconds is the maximum exposure you could use if you want sharp stars when using a 20mm lens on a full-frame camera. You then need to adjust the ISO for the correct exposure at this shutter speed and maximum aperture.

You will also need to research your subject, so you know when and where the core of the Milky Way or a good display of Northern Lights will be visible. Check out smartphone apps such as PhotoPills or forecast websites.

EXPOSURE BLENDING

If you have taken two shots (one exposed for the sky and a second for the foreground), you can blend these into a single shot containing the full range of tones. Open the two files in Photoshop and, using the Move Tool, drag the lighter one onto the darker one, where it will form a new layer (holding down the Shift key will ensure they are aligned). Click on the Add Layer Mask icon at the bottom of the Layers palette. Select a medium-sized, soft-edged brush, set the opacity to between 25 and 50 per cent, the foreground color to black, and gradually brush out the top layer of sky to reveal the darker one below.

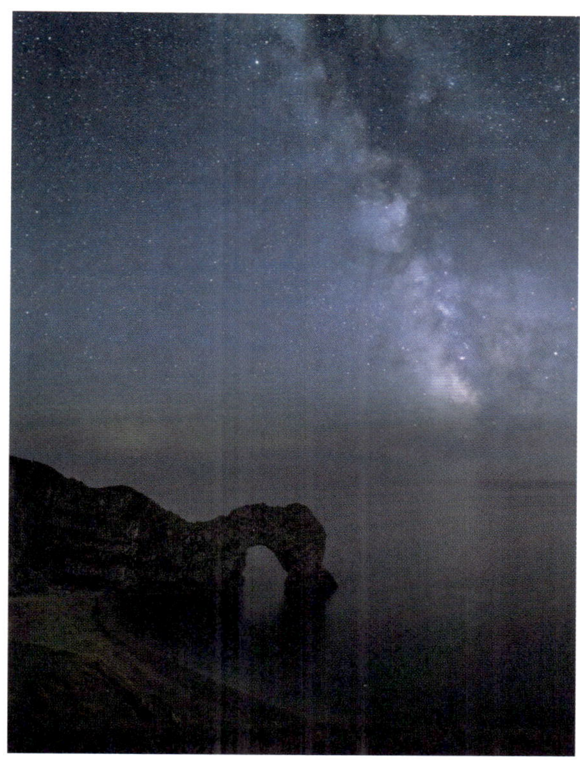

▲ *This Milky Way image was shot on a night with a new moon, with hardly any ambient light falling on the land below. To retain some detail in the land, a second, longer exposure was blended with the image of the night sky.*

FIELD NOTES

- You will need to compose and focus in complete darkness and calculate exposures when it is far too dark for your camera to meter the scene.

- It is easy to get seduced by the beauty of the stars or the Northern Lights, but a strong composition beneath the sky is just as important as it is with any landscape. However, it is not always easy to achieve.

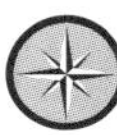

SPECIAL KIT

- Flashlight

- Tripod

- Lighting gel

TIPS

- Don't stand behind the camera—painting from the side will give more modeling to your subject.

- Lone trees, rock formations, and abandoned buildings all make great subjects.

- Try shooting when there is still a little color in the sky. After the blue hour, but before true darkness, is ideal.

- Base your exposure on a meter reading from the sky.

- To focus, shine your flashlight onto your subject and focus manually.

- If your flashlight is harsh and your subject close, try bouncing the light from a reflector.

FIELD NOTES

- Lock your shutter open in Bulb mode for the duration of the exposure and move the flashlight beam slowly and methodically around your subject.

- You can break the usual rules of night photography as cloud can add atmosphere to the scene. Light pollution can also benefit some images, by adding a sunset-like glow in the distance.

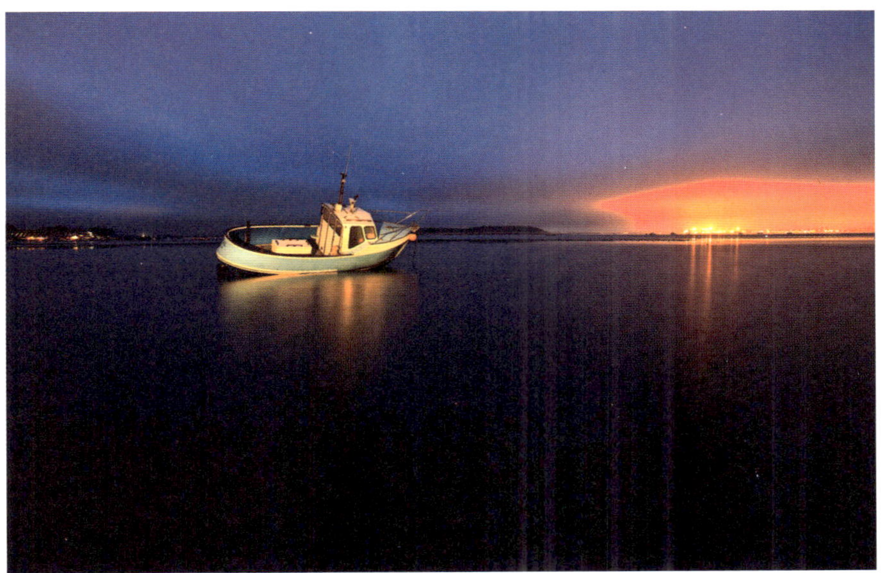

▲ *On a cloudy evening at the end of twilight, this boat was painted with a powerful flashlight for around half the duration of the 3 min. exposure.*

PAINT WITH LIGHT

If you enjoy nighttime photography, but have wondered what to do on cloudy evenings, this is the assignment for you. Painting with light is a technique in which you use a flashlight to subtly shine light on a subject, making it stand out from the rest of the scene, which will be in the relative darkness of the ambient light.

Painting with light works best if you keep it simple. Find a single subject—perhaps one that is naturally isolated—and paint that object only. Try to avoid over-painting, as your subject can appear too bright, and paint evenly. You probably won't need to shine the flashlight during the whole exposure, although exactly how long you should paint your subject for will depend on its distance from the light source, its size, and the brightness of your light. Begin by painting for about half the duration of the exposure, review your image, and then reshoot with more or less painting if necessary.

Most modern flashlights use LED lights, with brightness measured in lumens. There is no one correct brightness for light painting, so anything from 200 to 1,000 lumens could work, depending on subject distance; you just need to adjust how long you paint for. LEDs tend to produce a rather cool light, though, so you may want to use lighting gels to give the light a warmer tint.

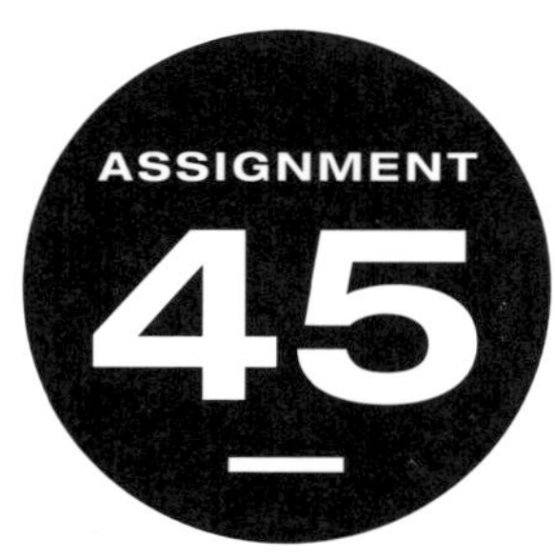

TIPS

- To create the best starburst effect, shoot in Manual or Aperture Priority exposure mode and select a small aperture, such as f/16.

- Shorter focal lengths are best for creating good starbursts, as (proportionally) the lens opening is smaller.

- Try partly obscuring the sun behind a solid object—the darker the area around the starburst, the more the light rays will stand out in your photo.

- Turn on your camera's highlights alert to check if you are losing any highlight detail—and apply negative exposure compensation if needed.

MAKE A STARBURST

A sun flare or starburst can really add sparkle and impact to your landscape images. This effect shows the sun, or any bright light source, as a near-perfect star, with rays of light radiating from the center. You can capture the effect using almost any camera type, but using an interchangeable lens camera—with adjustable aperture—will give you more control over the look of the final image.

The sunburst effect is the result of light diffraction, which is simply the bending and spreading of light waves. The smaller the opening that light passes through, the more light diffracts, so if you select a small aperture in the region of f/16 or f/22 you will exaggerate the effect. Experiment with different apertures, and go even smaller if necessary.

The number of rays from each starburst is related to the number of aperture blades in the lens being used. Typically, the more blades, the better the starburst. Diffraction will soften overall image quality, but it is worth it in this case for the creative effect. Your brief is to capture one great landscape image with a perfect starburst.

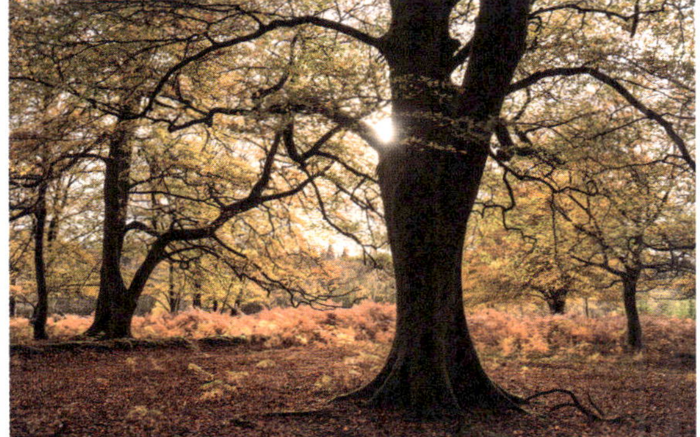

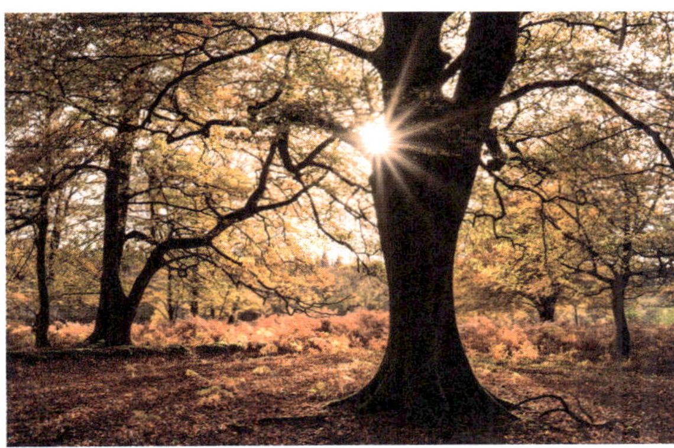

◄ *These images were taken just moments apart, the only difference being the aperture used. The photograph taken at f/22 (bottom) is far more dramatic than the one at f/8 (top), thanks to the effect and twinkle of a starburst.*

Achieving a good exposure can be difficult due to the high level of contrast caused by shooting into the light. Expect the very center of your starburst to be clipped and a small amount of highlight detail to be lost, but everything around it should be fine. If you are struggling for correct exposure, you can extend dynamic range by bracketing and merging two or more images together in post-processing (see page 103).

FIELD NOTES

- You may wish to capture the sun directly and unobstructed, but always take care when pointing a camera directly at the sun, as this can be harmful to your eyes.

- The risk of unwanted flare is enhanced when shooting toward the sun, so check that your lens and filters are spotlessly clean. You may still need to tidy up any undesired or colorful lens flare using the Clone or Healing Tool in post-processing.

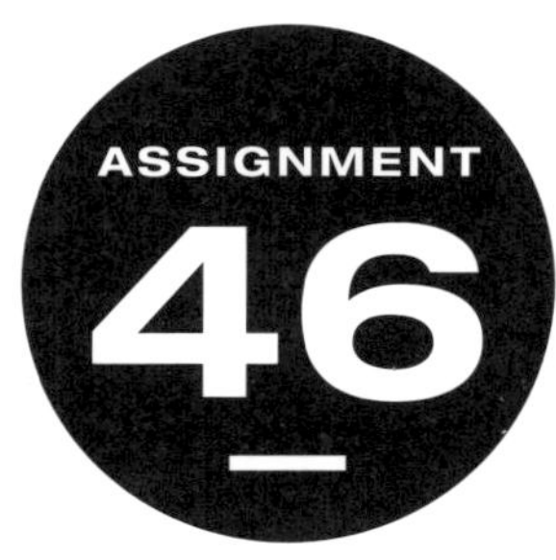

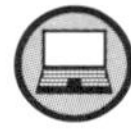

SPECIAL KIT

- Sturdy tripod

- Intervalometer

- Neutral density (ND) filter

- Post-processing software, such as Adobe Photoshop or Lightroom

TIPS

- Shoot in Raw to achieve a large dynamic range and to allow non-destructive adjustments in post-processing.

- Use large-capacity memory cards to avoid running out of memory before the sequence is complete.

- Use memory cards with a fast write speed to prevent the camera buffer filling up.

- To avoid flickering it is best to set the exposure in Manual mode.

- Try to keep your shutter speed below 1/50 sec. to keep the transition between frames smooth. If necessary, use a neutral density (ND) filter to achieve this.

- Ensure batteries are fully charged before you start and the sensor and lens are clean.

- Set White Balance manually for consistency throughout your sequence.

FIELD NOTES

You need movement and change to create interest, for example, the contrast of dark to light. No two scenes are alike, so you will need to experiment with the interval speed to get it just right; fast movement will require shorter intervals than slower-moving elements. To capture a rising or setting sun or a bustling urban landscape, an interval duration of 1–3 sec. is a good starting point.

▶ *Time-lapse sequences highlight change, contrast, and motion in the landscape.*

SPEED UP TIME

For this assignment you will be taking a break from shooting conventional still images. To convey time, movement, or change, it is better to capture a time-lapse sequence. This is a technique where you take a series of photos at regular intervals and then combine them into a continuous sequence to create a sped-up version of time. In this way you can compress hours (or even days) into just seconds or minutes. Time-lapse sequences can be a great way to highlight change, such as the sun rising and setting, the motion of waves, mist rolling over hills, or star trails.

As with any landscape photo, a strong composition is key. Scenes with a mix of dynamic and static elements work well. You only require a basic set-up to create a time-lapse video—a camera, a tripod, and an intervalometer (a device that triggers the camera at precise and regular intervals). Increasingly, cameras have this functionality built-in, and some even have a dedicated time-lapse function that will produce the video for you. You can also create basic time-lapse videos on your smartphone.

Your camera will need to be in a fixed position, and many advanced time-lapse photographers will employ auxiliary gadgets to introduce panning. Or, if you want more creative control, you can capture the frames and use dedicated software like Photoshop to organize and compile your sequence.

The number of images you need to take will depend on how long you want your time-lapse to be, but you will typically need 25 frames to create one second of footage (so a 30-second clip would need 750 frames). Trial and error will play a big part in creating a sequence.

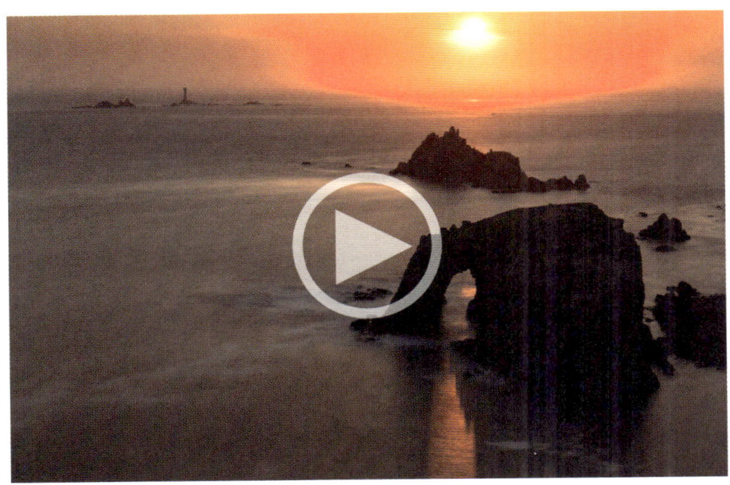

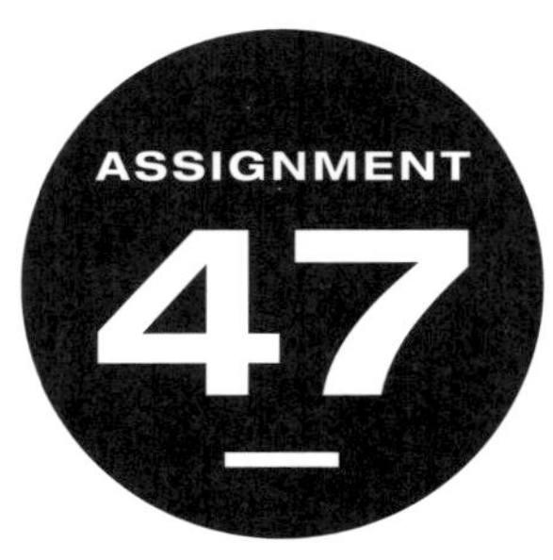

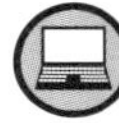

SPECIAL KIT

- Post-processing software, such as Adobe Photoshop

TIPS

- The ethereal soft glow created by sandwiching sharp and blurred images together, particularly suits back- and side-lit scenes, including mist, woodland, and any scene containing lots of foliage.

▶ *The Orton effect creates images that appear both highly detailed and soft and "dreamy." It is a distinctive look, with images having an almost fantasy style.*

LOSE FOCUS

For this assignment, we want you to lose focus! The "Orton Effect" is a popular creative style that gives images a bright, dreamlike glow. Abstract photographer Michael Orton first developed the technique in the 1980s in an attempt to imitate watercolor paintings. He did this by sandwiching two slides together of the same composition—one in focus and overexposed, another out of focus and underexposed—to create ethereal results. Today, we can easily replicate this effect using either in-camera multiple exposures, or with computer software (see overleaf).

Although it is easier and more precise to apply the effect post-capture, it is far more fun doing it in-camera. Simply select your camera's Multiple Exposure mode—this is typically found in your camera's Shooting Menu. Switch on Multiple Exposure and set the number of shots to two. Now, take your two frames. The first should be focused sharply as normal, but, for the second image, manually defocus the lens. The camera will then blend the sharp and blurred frames together to create one file. You will need to experiment with just how much you defocus the lens.

Enjoy this assignment. Apply the technique to a number of scenes, in different lighting conditions, to select the image where the effect works best.

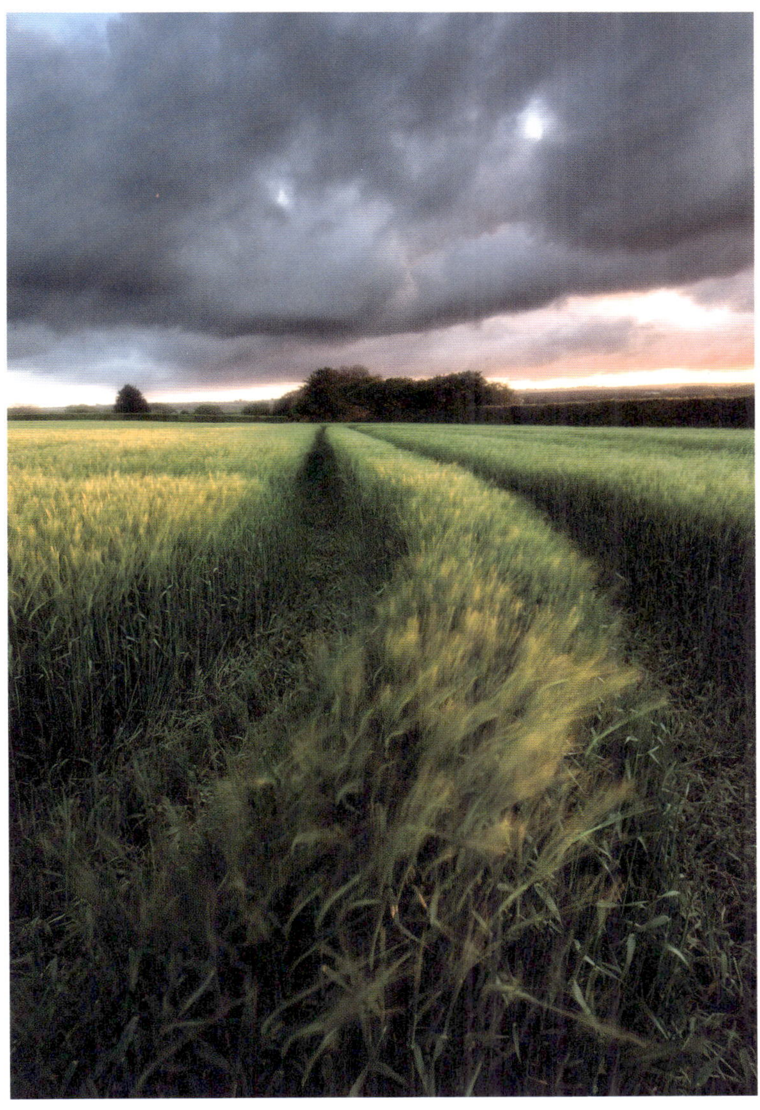

FIELD NOTES

If you are using your camera's built-in multiple exposure mode, set the overlay or blending method to "average" (or similar, depending on the camera make and model) to ensure the combined exposure is correct.

THE PROCESS

Although experimenting in the field is fun, creating the Orton Effect on your computer is quick, easy, and more precise. Photo-editing software, such as Photoshop, provides the ability to create a similar effect using just one image, and you can create or download a Photoshop Action to make the process even easier. The following is a quick and easy step-by-step.

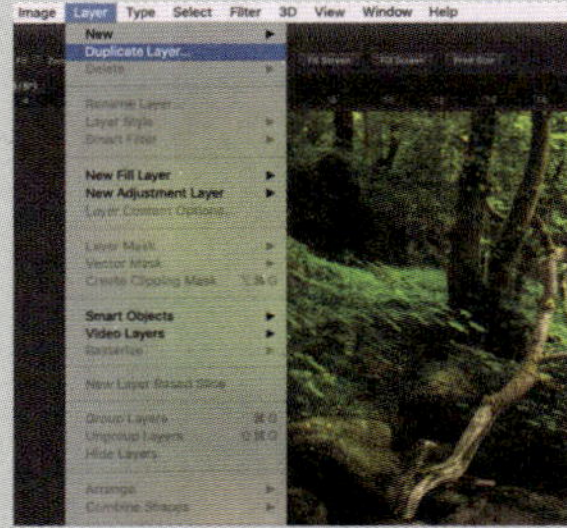

1 Select a suitable image and open it in Photoshop. Create a duplicate layer by clicking Layer > Duplicate Layer.

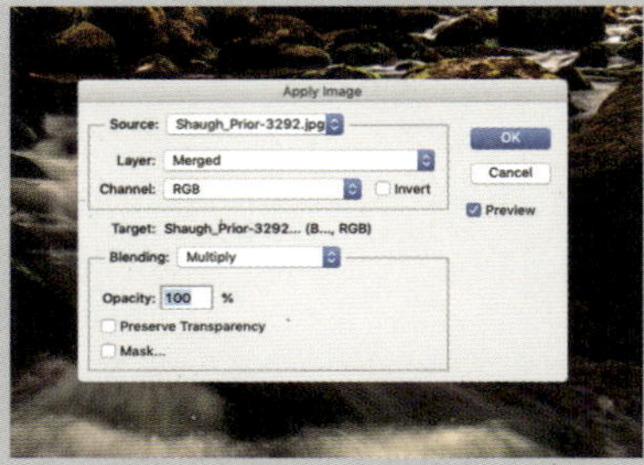

2 With your new layer selected, click Image > Apply Image. From the Blending dropdown menu, select Multiply and click OK. Your image should darken.

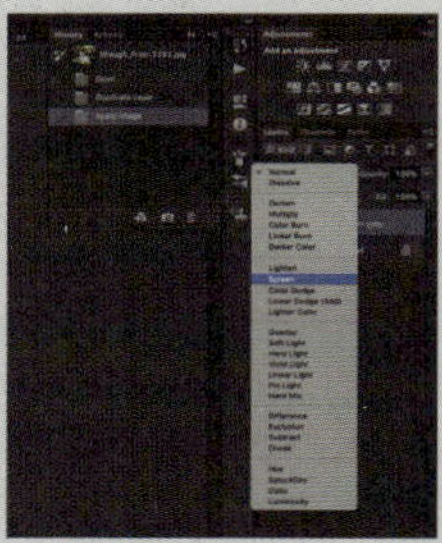

3 With your new layer still selected, alter the layer blend mode within the Layers window to Screen. Your image will return to its original brightness.

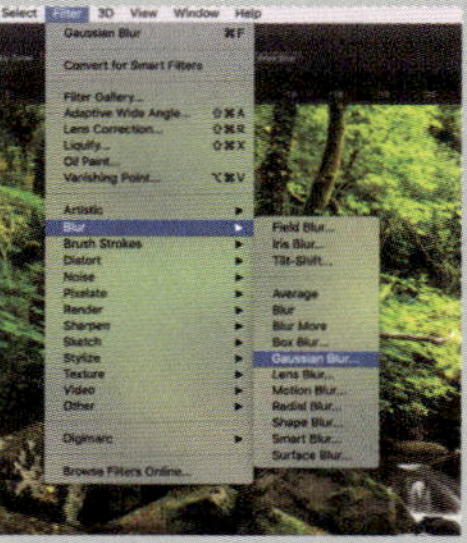

4 Click Filter > Blur and from the dropdown menu select Gaussian Blur. Use the slider to apply a medium amount of blur—in the region of 40–75 pixels. However, you will want to experiment with the level of blur, depending on the scene and the effect you wish to achieve. Now click OK to apply.

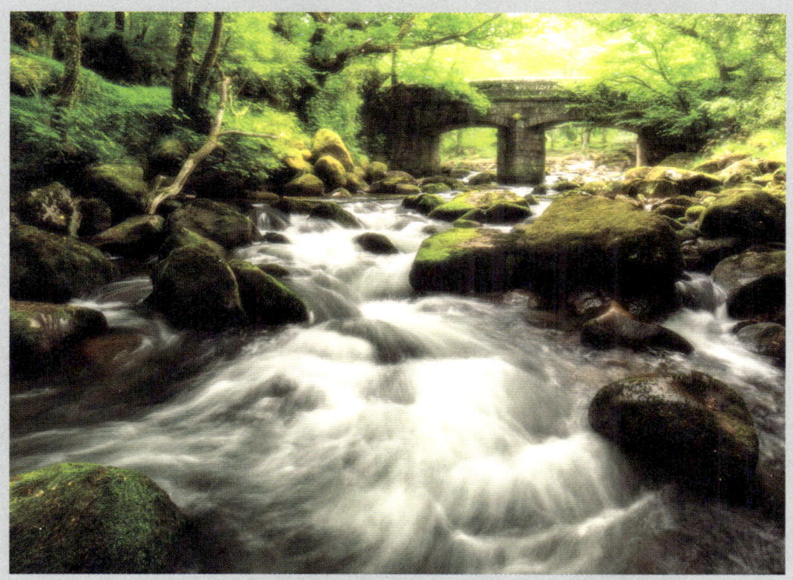

5 You will now see a dreamy softness and slight overexposure of the image's highlights. You can moderate the Orton Effect by adjusting the layer's Opacity in the Layers window. You may also need to readjust exposure by clicking Image > Adjustments > Levels.

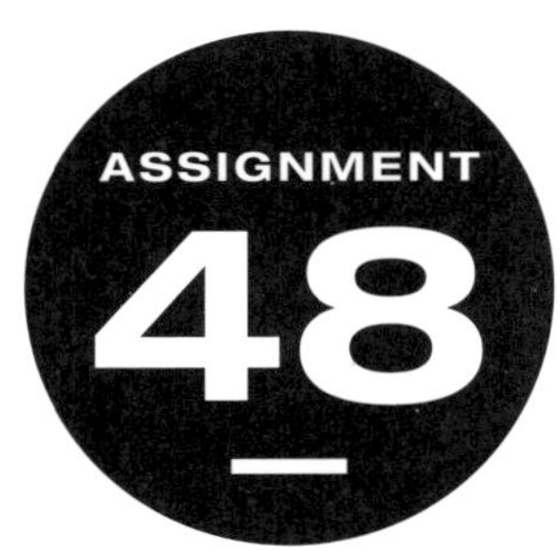

SPECIAL KIT

- Neutral density (ND) filter

TIPS

- Select a shutter speed of about 1 sec. and then move the camera during the exposure.

- Look for scenes with strong, recognizable shapes, colors, and contrast—trees work well, as can cityscapes, sunrises and sunsets, and beach scenes.

- You can use any focal length, but a short telephoto in the region of 60–100mm is often a good choice.

- Pan the camera smoothly. If you are struggling to do this handheld, use a tripod.

- You may need to attach a solid neutral density (ND) filter to artificially prolong exposure length.

MOVE IT

Intentional Camera Movement (ICM) is an abstract style of photography where the photographer deliberately moves the camera during the exposure to create an impressionistic interpretation of the landscape. Instead of taking a sharp photograph, you are effectively painting with your camera—nature provides the colors, textures, and interest, and the sensor becomes your canvas. This is a very subjective technique and you will either love or hate the results. Your assignment here has no rules—there is no definitive right or wrong, you simply need to capture an image that you like.

Shutter speed is the key to success here. Typically, an exposure length of 1–2 sec. works well, but experiment with different shutter speeds until you identify one that works best for you. To achieve an exposure of this length, select a low ISO and a small aperture.

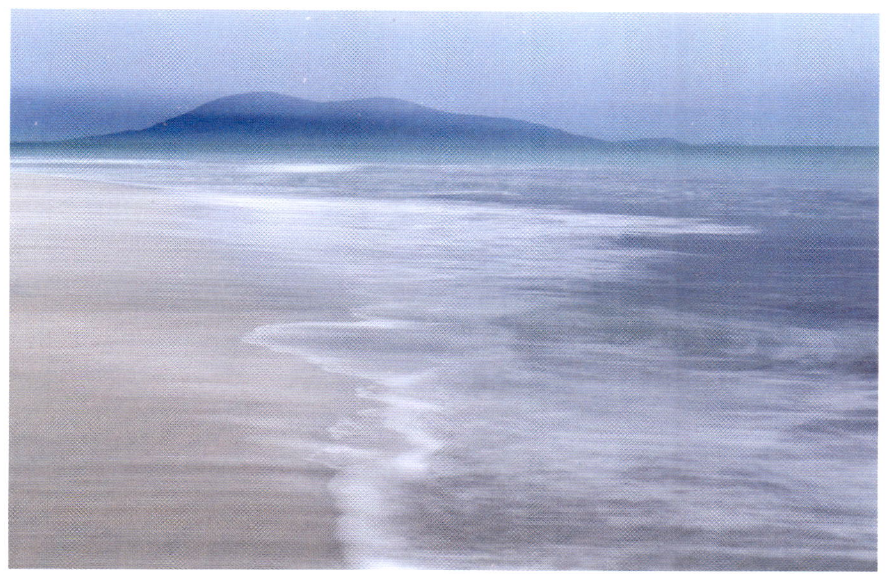

▲ *Contrast, color, and strong definition are important when taking this style of photograph.*

FIELD NOTES

This can be a very hit-and-miss style of photography and you may need to make many attempts before you achieve the level of motion and effect you desire.

Once you have identified a subject, begin slowly panning the camera—vertically or horizontally, depending on the type of scene—and then gently trigger the shutter while continuing to pan in one smooth, flowing motion.

Be patient—it can take countless attempts to get a photo you like. Different types of movement will yield very different results. Although dragging the camera vertically or horizontally is most popular, rotating the camera or moving it back and forth during exposure can also produce eye-catching images.

The most important thing with this assignment is to have fun experimenting!

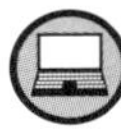

SPECIAL KIT

- Post-processing software, such as Adobe Photoshop

TIPS

- Choosing the right picture is important—this effect works best with shots with a wide field of view, looking down from a high angle. Simple scenes are a good choice for this technique, especially cityscapes.

- Everything in the original photograph should be sharp, as you will be adding blur to it.

SHRINK THINGS DOWN

Tilt-shift lenses are best known in landscape photography for generating extensive depth of field and keeping vertical lines straight. Another use for them is to create the "miniature" effect, where a scene is photographed so that it appears as if a scale model has been shot from close range using a macro lens. This has traditionally been achieved by using the movements of a tilt-shift lens to severely restrict the depth of field in the scene. You will almost certainly have seen this effect before as the style has become popular in film and TV for short clips of urban scenes.

Fortunately, you don't need to splash out on expensive tilt-shift lenses to complete this assignment—you can achieve the effect with relative ease in post-processing on your computer, using software such as Adobe Photoshop (see overleaf). All you need is the right shot to begin with. Scale models often use very bright paint, so, to further simulate this look, you can increase color saturation. Don't worry about going too far—this is one occasion where you really don't need to keep things looking natural!

◄ Cars, trains, boats, and other vehicles make excellent subjects for the tilt-shift miniature treatment.

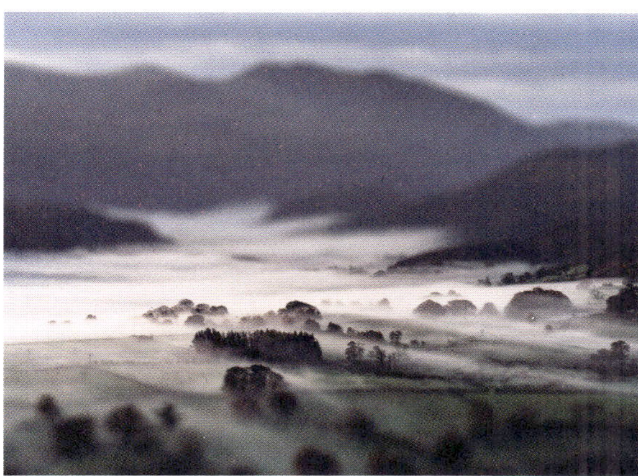

◄ Although more associated with cityscapes, this effect can also work with rural landscapes—in this example, the tall trees help make the technique successful.

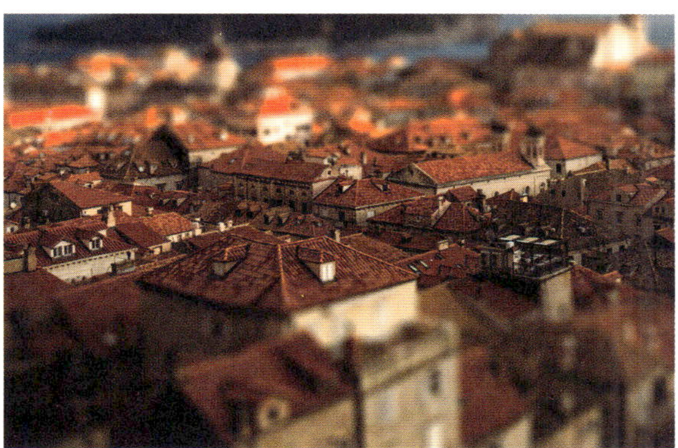

◄ City views, especially with the sky cropped out of the frame, can also look good when given the miniature treatment.

THE PROCESS

Creating the miniature effect is great fun, and a good way to while away some time on a rainy day when you can't get out with the camera. Simply follow the steps below in Adobe Photoshop.

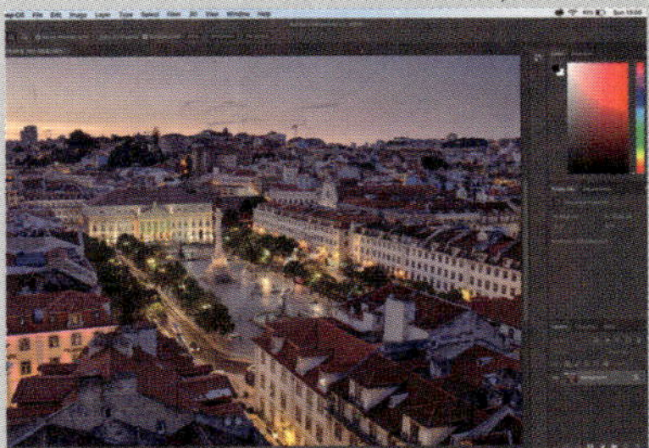

1 Choose a suitable picture and open it in Photoshop.

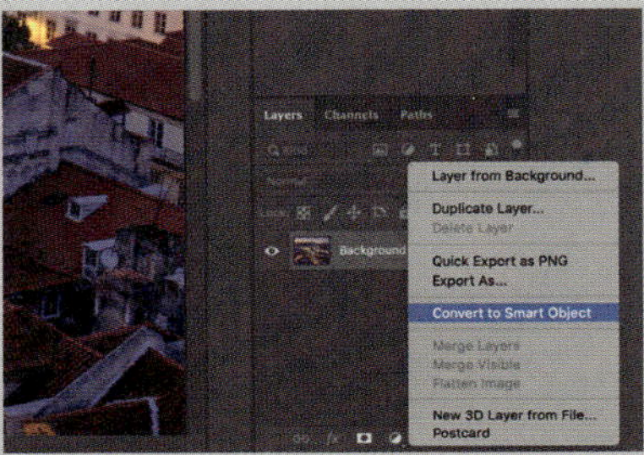

2 Right-click the background layer and choose Convert to Smart Object. Smart objects are useful when using filters, as they make the applied filters editable at any time.

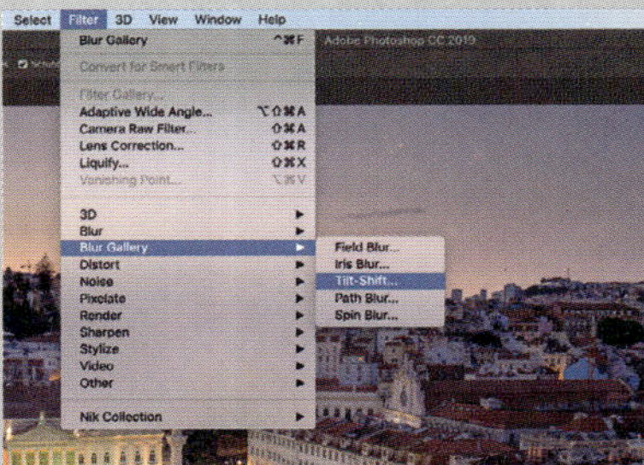

3 Go to Filter > Blur Gallery > Tilt-Shift to activate the filter.

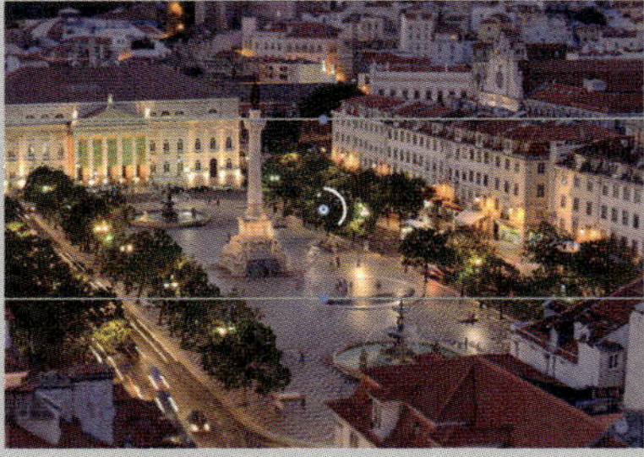

4 You will see a pin in the middle of the image with solid lines either side of it, and dashed lines above and below them. The filter effect will be previewed with default values. The area inside the solid lines is the "protected area," which has no filter effect applied. The "transition areas" are between the solid lines and the dashed lines—blur increases progressively toward the dashed lines, where it reaches full strength. Beyond the dashed lines, the filter effect is applied fully.

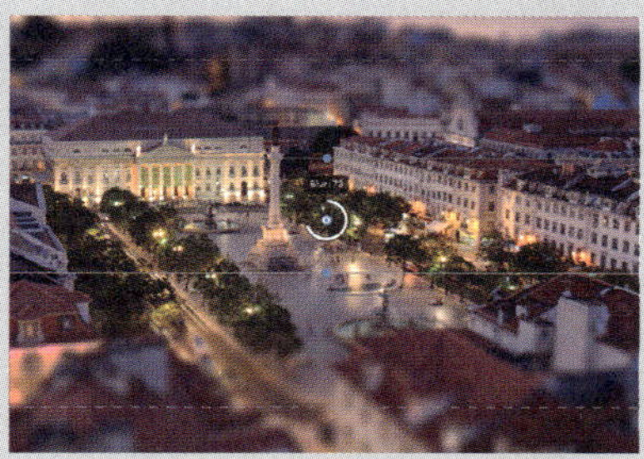

5 Adjust the amount of blur by clicking on the ring outside the central pin. Drag it clockwise to increase it or counterclockwise to decrease it. Adjust the size of the protected area by clicking and dragging the solid lines, and adjust the transition area by clicking and dragging the dashed lines. To move the protected area, click inside and drag. To adjust its orientation, click on one of the blue dots on the solid lines. Click OK above the image to apply the filter.

6 To make things look even more like a scale model than a real scene, you can increase the color saturation, as I have done for this final image.

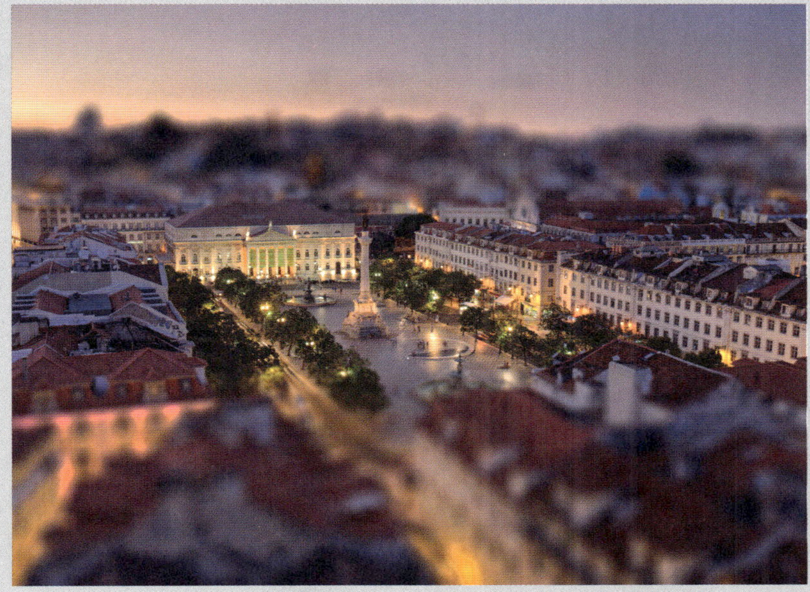

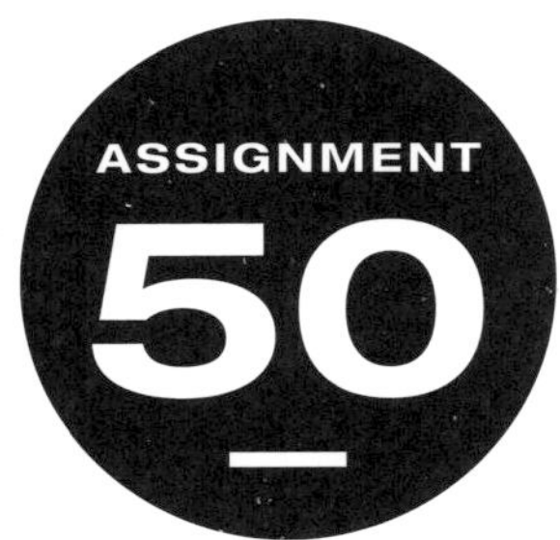

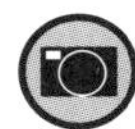

SPECIAL KIT

- Post-processing software, such as Adobe Photoshop

TIPS

- Scenes with tall or colorful structures, or a relatively uniform bottom or top part (like a sky or river), tend to work best.

- If you are not using a 360-degree panorama, select images where the left and right edges of the image are similar to help disguise the join where the two ends meet.

- The sky will be severely distorted. Clear skies tend to produce the best results, although clouds can give an interesting, stretched effect.

SMALL WORLDS

It is important to have fun with your photography, and that is exactly what this assignment is designed for. Ideally, you will have already completed Assignment 16 (see page 44) and created a stitched panoramic image. Now, let's go one step further and transform your panorama into a shot resembling a miniature planet. This technique is known as stereographic projection and the results are fun, novel, and eye-catching.

Virtually any panoramic image can be turned into a little globe, but 360-degree stitches work best as their edges should align almost seamlessly. The photograph's aspect ratio will affect how the planet appears. Wider images tend to produce smoother planet surfaces, while narrower panoramas give more height variation. Both can look great.

THE PROCESS

Using this simple Adobe Photoshop step-by-step, you will soon be creating your very own globe effect shots.

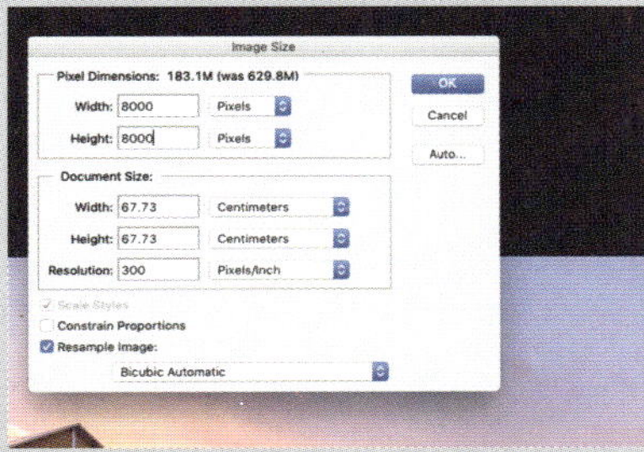

1 First, you need to make your panoramic image into a square. Click Image > Image Size. Uncheck Constrain Proportions and set the height to match the width. This will squash your image into a square.

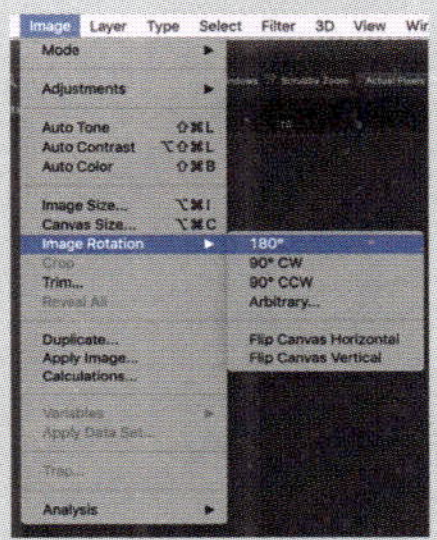

2 Flip your image upside down by clicking Image > Image Rotation > 180°. This will help ensure it wraps the right way when transformed into a planet.

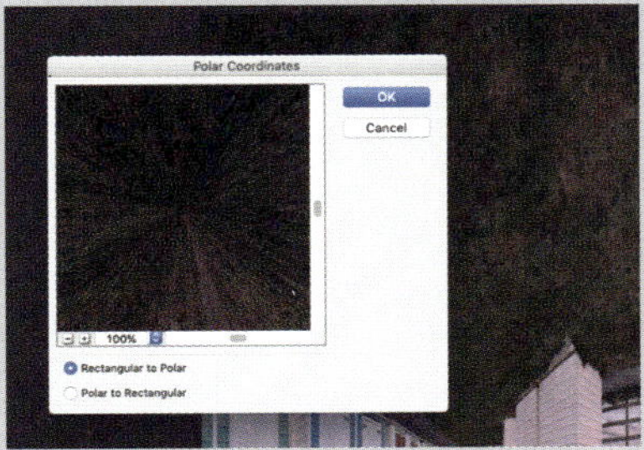

3 Next, go to Filter > Distort > Polar Coordinates. Select the Rectangular to Polar option and click OK.

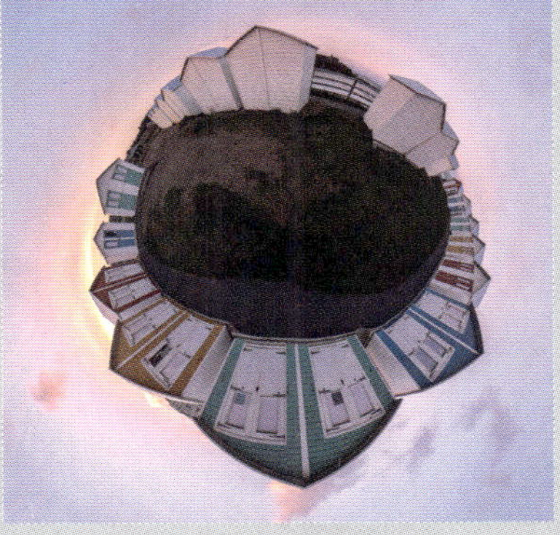

4 You have now created a stereographic projection—a panorama wrapped into a circle that should resemble a tiny planet photographed from above using a fisheye lens. Check where the edges join and use the Clone or Healing Brush to smooth any untidy areas. You might also decide to rotate or crop the image to achieve the best result.

SPECIAL KIT

- Post-processing software, such as Adobe Photoshop

- Inkjet printer

- Colorimeter for monitor color calibration, such as DataColor Spyder

TIPS

- The first step in producing a good print is to calibrate your monitor so that you know that the colors you are seeing are accurate—this is done using a hardware colorimeter.

- For an accurate screen-to-print match, you will also need to download paper profiles. Custom profiles are not expensive and free generic profiles are available to download from the paper manufacturers' websites.

- If you are inexperienced with color management, there are plenty of online tutorials—an elementary internet search will reveal a wealth of material.

- If you are really not confident, you can always outsource your printing to a professional lab, who will handle the color management for you.

PRINT IT

These days, far too many pictures just languish on computer hard drives and never see the light of day. But go back just two or three decades and most serious photography enthusiasts were busy in darkrooms, producing prints of their favorite work. Darkroom printing is not an easy process, and involves chemicals and trial and error, and is not 100 per cent repeatable. These days, printing is far more accessible and consistent. You don't need much space—just a desk with a computer and an inkjet printer. The hardware doesn't have to be expensive or as specialist as traditional darkroom equipment.

For this project you should choose your favorite image from the assignments you have followed in this book and produce an outstanding print that you can display in your home. The key to making an accurate print is the process of soft-proofing. This is where, in software, you create an on-screen representation of how your image will appear on your chosen paper. It will differ from the original on-screen image because paper and ink have a narrower color gamut and contrast range than your computer monitor. You can then make adjustments to the print to match it as closely as possible to the original image. It's not a difficult process, but it's worth finding some online tutorials or reading an in-depth article on digital printing before you begin.

The classic way of displaying photographs is in a frame with a "window mount." There are, however, many other options, including canvas wraps, aluminum prints, and acrylic prints. Even if your end product is a traditional framed print there are many different paper types to choose from, ranging from glossy resin-coated paper to textured "fine art" paper. It can be worth experimenting to see which suits your image best—many manufacturers sell test packs for this purpose.

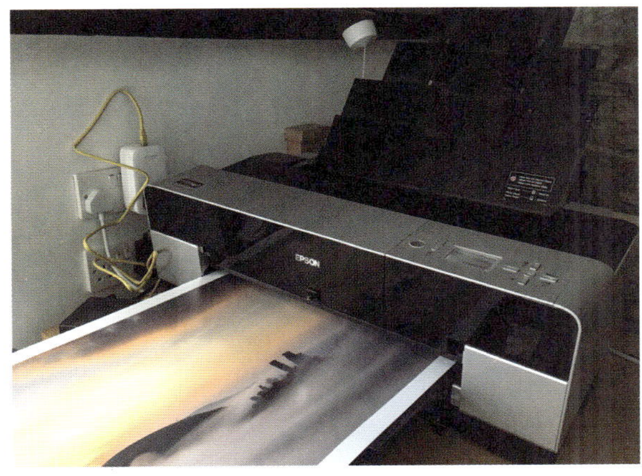

◀ *For some photographers, a photograph doesn't exist until you make a print of it.*

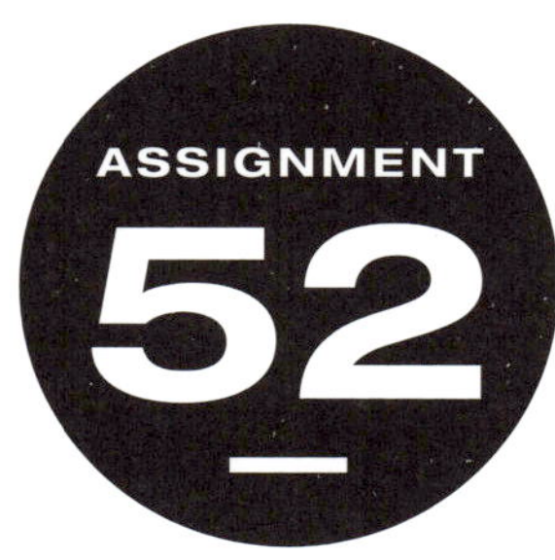

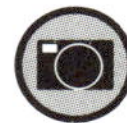
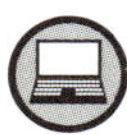

SPECIAL KIT

- Website software or builder, such as Photium, Smugmug, Squarespace, Wix, or Wordpress

- Website domain name, purchased from registrar, such as GoDaddy or Namecheap

TIPS

- Creating a blog that shares your thoughts and adventures is helpful for improved Search Engine Optimization (SEO). This means that more visitors are attracted to your site through Google, for instance, as a result of regularly updated content.

- Add a Contact Page, so people—including those who may be interested in buying your photographs—can connect with you.

- Make sure you include links on your website to any social media pages you also have.

▼ ▶ The best sites look clean and simple. Keep your accompanying text concise and punchy—let your images do the talking.

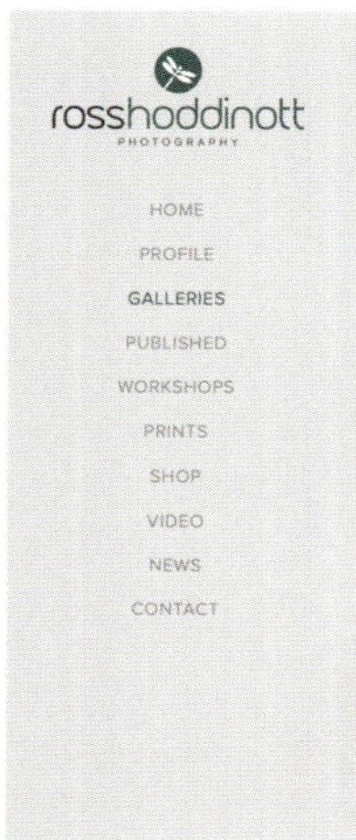

The Land

This collection of landscape photographs is dedicated to The Land – photos of mountains, moorland, heathland, rivers, woodland and rolling countryside. The scenery is the UK is as diverse as it is beautiful, and Ross's images capture the very essence, mood and character of the British landscape. All photographs are available to buy as FINE ART PRINTS. Just click on the shopping bag icon below any gallery image to view print options and cost. To learn more about our prints, paper-types and delivery, visit our PRINTS page. Images are also available for commercial license – please contact us with your requirements.

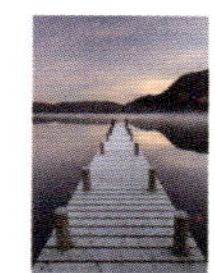
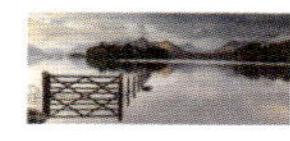
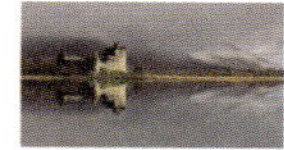
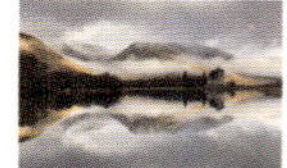
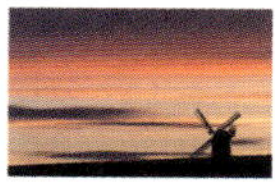

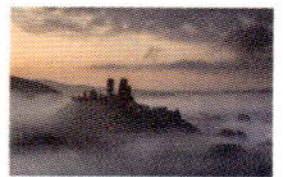
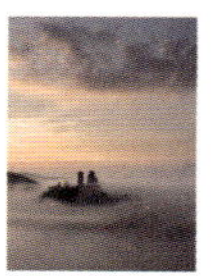

GO LIVE

Having captured all these wonderful landscape images, don't keep them hidden away on your computer's hard drive. For this assignment, you need to create a platform to share your photographs. Most of us don't have the time or skill to build a customized website from scratch, but that's okay—you don't need to be particularly computer-literate to create your own online portfolio.

The easiest option is to use a website builder. Although you have to pay, the cost for a basic site and hosting is relatively inexpensive and within hours your photographs can be seen, enjoyed, and even purchased, by anyone, anywhere. Photium, Smugmug, Squarespace, Wix, and Wordpress are among the best website builders for photographers. They offer hundreds of templates and intuitive drag-and-drop systems to keep the process of creating your site quick and simple. Most pages are easy to customize, too, so you can make your site look distinctive.

Don't overload your galleries with images. This should be a showcase for your landscape photography, so only publish your very best shots—you only have one chance to make a good first impression. The more streamlined your portfolio, the more effective it will be. Once your site is live, the assignment is complete.

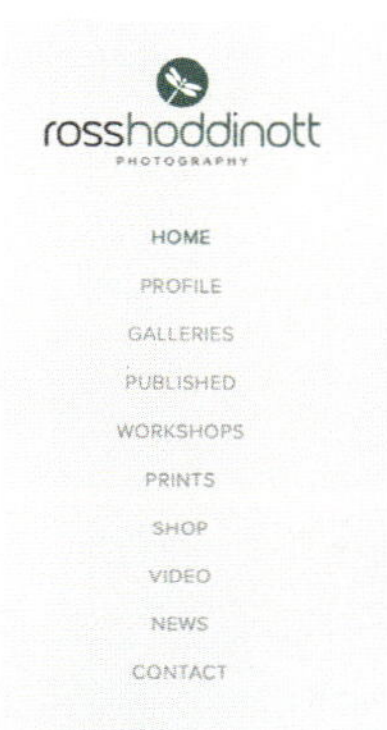

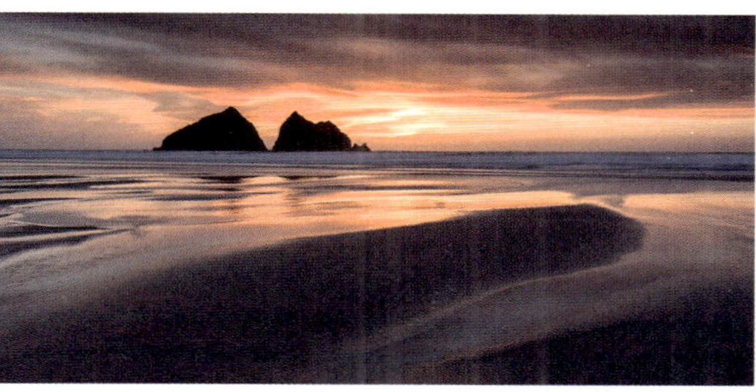

FIELD NOTES

You will need to purchase a domain name for your site—typically your name, or your name followed by photography, for example, "joebloggsphotography.com". Visit a registrar, such as GoDaddy or Namecheap. You can normally buy a domain for a small annual fee.

INDEX